ENGLISH GRAMMAR

a functional approach

JOHN COLLERSON

Primary English Teaching Association

National Library of Australia Cataloguing-in-Publication data

Collerson, John
English grammar: a functional approach

Bibliography
Includes index
ISBN 1 875622 11 X

1. English language – Grammar.   I. Primary English Teaching Association
(Australia). II. Title.

425

First published October 1994
Reprinted May 1995
Copyright © Primary English Teaching Association 1994
Laura Street Newtown NSW 2042 Australia
Cover based on a stage design by Ferdinando Bibiena (1711)
Designed by Anne-Marie Rahilly and Jeremy Steele
Edited by Jeremy Steele
Index prepared by Garry Cousins
Typeset in 10.5/12.5 Palatino at the Training and Development Centre
Cnr The Boulevarde and Toothill Street Lewisham NSW 2049
Printed by Ambassador Press
51 Good Street Granville NSW 2142

Foreword

English Grammar: A Functional Approach is a somewhat unusual publishing venture for PETA, but one that is very important within today's changing context of primary English teaching. It is not a practical teaching resource — you will not find in it the detailed suggestions and strategies for classroom implementation that PETA readers have come to expect from most of our books. Rather it is a reference for teachers, a contribution to your knowledge of the English language and how it functions.

PETA is well regarded for its commitment to professional development and for keeping teachers abreast of new developments in the field of primary English. The functional approach to studying and teaching English is one we have progressively introduced to our members. Several years ago, John Collerson's *Writing for Life* showed how teachers could build upon the gains achieved in a process approach to writing by focusing on various written genres. Subsequently, Beverly Derewianka's *Exploring How Texts Work*, a PETA best-seller, demonstrated how teachers could help children to develop effective texts for particular purposes, within the context of purposeful and stimulating language use. Both books have stressed the need for teachers and children to share a 'language for talking about language'.

It is now widely accepted that to become more critical readers and effective writers, primary children do need to learn how to explore texts and talk about how they work to make meaning. To do so, they need a grammar that shows them how their language operates as a resource for making meaning and that helps them to make informed choices as writers and speakers. A functional grammar does just this.

However, before teachers can make use of a functional grammar in the classroom, they must themselves feel comfortable with their knowledge of it. PETA believes that the best way we can help teachers gain such knowledge is to publish a book that is both sufficiently detailed to explain the grammar clearly and sufficiently accessible for readers not to need a degree in linguistics to understand it. This is such a book, written by someone highly respected for his knowledge in the field and his understanding of teachers and their needs. We are confident that you will find it a genuinely interesting and readable reference text that will help you to develop your knowledge of language.

It is not a 'quick-fix' book to read at one sitting, but one to read in sections, to return to, to consult via the index, and to discuss with your colleagues over a period of time. It should be viewed as a long-term professional development resource.

Over the next couple of years we will be publishing other materials that will help teachers to use the grammar to inform their language planning and programming, and help them develop in children a more explicit knowledge of how their language operates. We strongly believe, however, that the first step is for teachers to become better acquainted with a functional approach to English grammar, and in that belief we are proud to publish this book.

Kerrie Scott
President

Contents

Preface

This book has been written to provide teachers and teacher education students with an introduction to English grammar based on a functional approach. It is not intended as a grammar for teaching directly to school students but rather as a guide for teachers themselves. However, some of the ways in which texts and examples are discussed may provide teachers with ideas which can be adapted for classroom use, depending on the level and previous experience of the students.

Readers familiar with some traditional grammar will find this functional approach a little different, but they will soon begin to recognise familiar landmarks. A lot of traditional grammar (nouns, verbs, clauses and so on) is included here, and so some knowledge of traditional grammar will not go astray. However, this is not just traditional grammar with the names changed; it has a different basis. So if you are not familiar with any kind of grammar, that will not matter. You will be able to approach this kind with a fresh outlook and take in everything as it is gradually explained.

A functional approach to grammar is concerned with how language works to achieve various purposes. It takes account of how the contexts in which language is used and the purposes of the users give rise to particular texts. It is based on the functional components of texts and the meanings they embody, rather than on the words and structures which express those meanings. The local details of word form and structure have an important place in the grammar, but they are best understood in terms of the way they fit into larger functional components which can be directly related to the meanings being expressed.

Moreover, while traditional grammar is based very much on written English and on more formal uses of language, this approach includes features of grammar that are relevant mainly to the spoken language, including informal conversation. Nevertheless it is equally applicable to written English, and many of the examples in the following chapters are drawn from written texts.

The reason teachers should know something about grammar is not so that they can teach it all to their students in a systematic way — or not necessarily. There is a difference between what a teacher knows and what the teacher might teach to students. Furthermore, it is not necessary for children (or anyone) to know the grammar in order to be able to use the language. But if teachers have some knowledge of grammar, it can help them to understand how language is being used and to talk with children about their use of it. And as teachers develop their own understanding of the language, they can gradually move from the commonsense terms in which they might at first talk about language towards a more informed, refined and systematic understanding.

The teacher's systematic knowledge of the grammar then becomes a resource to draw on in talking with children about their writing or other uses of language. A functional grammar is more appropriate for teachers than traditional grammar (even though they have a good deal in common) because a functional grammar can be more directly related to the ways in which students use language. Its implications for the classroom are further explored in the Postscript.

The approach adopted here is based mainly on the work of M. A. K. Halliday, especially his *Introduction to Functional Grammar* (1985), though it differs from it in some respects. It also owes something to other modern grammars, including G. Leech and J. Svartvik, *A Communicative Grammar of English* (1975).

I would like to thank Michael Halliday for his interest and encouragement. I am especially grateful to Jim Martin and Ray Werren, who each provided detailed comments on an earlier draft of the text. I have also had the opportunity of learning from and discussing grammar with many other people, including John Carr, Beverly Derewianka, Ruqaiya Hasan, Joan Rothery, Len Unsworth, Geoff Williams and Bill Winser. I have received much encouragement and support from colleagues at the University of Western Sydney, especially Bronwyn Beecher, John Grierson and Richard Parker at Macarthur, and Helen Farrell and Joanne Tiernan at Nepean. However, while I am indebted to all these people, I have not always followed their advice and I must accept responsibility for the way the grammar is presented here.

I would also like to thank Thurley Fowler and Lansdowne Publishing for permission to include an extended extract from *The Green Wind* in Chapter 9. Finally, I would like to express my gratitude to two people at PETA, Vivienne Nicoll and Jeremy Steele, who have worked so hard to bring this book to publication.

J. C.

Grammar and the Functions of Language

Grammar is something which attracts the attention of a variety of people in the community — teachers, parents, academics, politicians, talk-show hosts, writers to the editor and guardians of good taste. It arouses interest, concern and controversy. However, not everyone's idea of grammar is the same, and so first we should clarify what it means to us. Yet it's not really grammar alone that should be the focus of our attention, but language — in this case, the English language. For grammar is not some isolated system with a life of its own; it is an integral part of language.

Our language isn't an isolated system either. It is part of our culture and way of life — something that we share with others. It is largely through language that we take part in the life of our community and the wider society to which we belong. The purposes we have for using language and the meanings we express come from the social context, and our language is organised to serve social functions. These are reflected in the grammar, which is central to the organisation of language. So, before we consider how different kinds of meaning are expressed through particular parts of the grammar, we should look at how grammar and language are related to the wider social context.

What is grammar?

We can best think of grammar as the way a language is organised. Whenever we use language — in speaking or listening, in writing, reading or just thinking — we select and arrange the words and other components in certain ways, according to certain principles, though usually we're not aware of doing so. It is this organisation which enables us to achieve all the various purposes for which we use language.

However, it's not just grammar that's involved, but also what is called the **lexicon** or vocabulary of the language — the stock of words and other meaningful elements, such as parts of words and idiomatic expressions, which makes up the material to be organised. The grammar and the lexicon form one system: that is, the **lexicogrammatical** system.

Our language (or languages, if we use more than one) has a central role in our lives, which can be described in terms of three very general functions:

Action   Language is a way of acting upon the world, allowing us to take part in the activities of life and to interact with the people around us. It is 'part of the action'.

Reflection   Language reflects our experience of the world — we can think of it as a representation of the world. At the same time it enables us to reflect on our experience and make sense of the world.

Connection   Language provides us with the means of showing the connections between any text and its context, as well as connections within the text.

How these three major functions are realised through the organisation of the language will become clearer as we explore the grammar in the examples discussed in this and subsequent chapters. However, before plunging into details of the grammar, let's take a step back and see how it is related to the social context.

Grammar in text and context

Language is involved in almost everything we do. It influences our whole view of the world, because it is largely through language that we make sense of our experience. Some of the things we do are actually constituted through language — they come into existence through our use of language. With other things, the language accompanies the activities and shapes the way we think about them.

Whenever we use language there is a context. The immediate context is the situation in which the language is being used. But every situation is also part of the larger culture in which we live. This **context of culture** — the broad sphere of our operations — involves shared meanings and assumptions; it allows us to take certain things for granted. We must recognise too that within the Australian community there are different cultures and languages; many specific situations involve the interplay of different cultural assumptions.

Within the broad context of culture (or cultures), the immediate context of any particular occasion of language use — what is called the **context of situation** — can be characterised by three features:

the **tenor** of the relationship between the people involved (e.g. mother-child, teacher-pupil, fellow team-members, friends), the 'tone' of the language and the attitudes and feelings embodied in the language the **field** of human activity which is involved (e.g. domestic activities – cooking, cleaning, caring for children; commerce – shopping, banking; recreation – music, football, etc.)

the **mode** of language use: that is, the role being played by the language itself (e.g. whether spoken or written, face-to-face conversation, reading aloud, etc., and also whether the language is part of the current activity or reflects something else).

The meanings which are communicated and the kind of language being used are determined largely by these features of the context and by the specific purposes that people have in using language (which often arise from the context itself). The way these features are related to the three major functions of language can be indicated in a diagram:

Features of context	Major functions of language	
	informal term	*formal term*
tenor	action	interpersonal
field	reflection	experiential *or* ideational
mode	connection	textual

We'll now begin to explore all this by considering two texts, one of written English and the other a transcript of spoken English. They will help to show us how the language features of a text are related to its context and how the functions of language are expressed in the grammar.

A written text

TEXT 1.1 A NOTICE AND PERMISSION NOTE FOR A SCHOOL EXCURSION

HOPETOUN VALE PUBLIC SCHOOL

Mountain View Road
Hopetoun Vale

15th November 1993

Dear Parents,

On Thursday, 25th November 1993, the children in 5G will be visiting Taronga Park Zoo as part of their Science and Social Studies units of work on Endangered Species and Hot-Wet Lands.

The excursion will cost $10.50. This will cover the bus to Circular Quay, the ferry to Taronga and entrance into the Zoo.

Children will be departing school at 8.45 am, and returning by 3.30 pm.

Children are required to wear full school uniform and bring their lunch in a throwaway bag. Spending money is optional and there is a maximum limit of $5.00.

J. R. TYLER   B. GORDON
Principal   5G Teacher

‒ ‒

Permission Note

I hereby give my permission for my son/daughter .... to attend the excursion to Taronga Park Zoo on 25.11.93.

Signed ....
Parent/Guardian

We can say several things about the context of Text 1.1, using the notions of field, tenor and mode:

Field   General: education. Specific: primary schooling, school excursions, arranging a school excursion.

Tenor   The text is addressed to a particular group of parents and it is from 'the school' as an institution, represented by the principal and the class teacher. The signatories to the notice and the parents have distinct roles and there are fairly clear expectations about the kind of relationship that exists amongst them.
   The permission note provides the parents with pre-arranged wording for responding to the notice.

Mode   The mode is written English in the form of a photocopied notice sent home with the children and incorporating a tear-off slip for response.

These features characterise the situational context in which the text has arisen. The meanings explicit in the text come directly from the context; they include the purposes of the text, who it's addressed to and who it's from. For this text, like any other, plays a part in the life of these people: it is part of the action — one of the steps in the process of arranging the excursion. At the same time, it depicts part of the world in which the people live and operate. How does all this come out in the grammar and vocabulary of the text?

The grammar of action
The authors of the text have several reasons for sending it, which help to determine the grammatical choices they make. Another factor which

influences these choices is the relationship that exists between the school and the parents: that is, the tenor of this situation.

The main part of the text is both informative and directive. It sets out all the arrangements for the excursion that the parents need to know and does this in a very definite way, with a tone of authority:

> the children in 5G will be visiting Taronga Park Zoo . . .
>
> The excursion will cost $10.50.
>
> Children are required to wear full school uniform . . .

You can see how grammatical and lexical choices make a difference to the 'tone' of a text (reflecting a different purpose) if you consider other possibilities:

> We're thinking of taking the kids in 5G to the Zoo.
>
> The excursion will probably cost about $10 or $11.
>
> We'd like the children to wear their school uniforms.

The permission note itself has a legal purpose: namely, to provide the school with written evidence that each child has a parent's permission to go on the excursion. The wording (*I hereby give my permission . . .*) is a legal convention that's unlikely to occur in speech or in writing for other purposes.

A reflection of the world

This text emerges from a particular field of activity which is part of the world these people experience, as is evident in such elements of the wording as *school, the children, the excursion, Taronga Park Zoo* or *their lunch*. These are all 'things' associated with this field of activity, but there are other things in the text which are more complex and require a more elaborate grammatical structure — for example:

> the ferry to Taronga   a throwaway bag
>
> entrance into the Zoo   spending money
>
> full school uniform   a maximum limit of $5.00

or even something as elaborate as:

> part of their Science and Social Studies units of work on Endangered Species and Hot-Wet Lands.

With these examples (even the short ones), we can begin to see how the choice of language actually brings some aspects of this world into existence. The people experience their world through the language. One example in particular illustrates the way in which the grammatical and lexical resources of the language are used to shape our experience: *a throwaway bag* clearly denotes 'a bag which can be thrown away', but in our fast-moving society most of that longer expression is 'repackaged' as one word, *throwaway*, which becomes a new kind of classification. The same tendency can be seen in expressions like *takeaway food, a slip-on cover* and *a tear-off slip*. I'm not implying that this is a good or bad thing — simply that it is one of the ways we have of using the grammatical resources of the language.

The world of experience consists not only of things but also of processes, including actions such as:

> visiting, departing, returning, wear(ing), bring(ing)

Less active processes are evident in these examples:

> The excursion *will cost* . . .
>
> This *will cover* . . .
>
> Children *are required* to wear . . .

Another kind of process is a state of affairs, represented by the word *is*:

> Spending money *is* optional and there *is* a maximum limit . . .

One further aspect of the world which we represent in language is the circumstances in which everything goes on. In this text they are mainly circumstances of time and place, and most of them are quite specific:

> On Thursday, 25th November 1993
>
> at 8.45 am   by 3.30 pm
>
> in a throwaway bag

All these things (the purposes, the people, the actions and the picture of the world) are presented to us partly through the individual words but more particularly in the way the words are organised. It is this organisation, and the principles that govern it, which we refer to as grammar.

A spoken text

It would be a mistake to think that grammar applies only to written language, for when we speak, we are still drawing on the lexical and grammatical resources of the language (though not always in the same way). So let's now consider a text derived from spoken English.

TEXT 1.2 A TRANSCRIPT OF A CONVERSATION BETWEEN THREE ADULTS

Geoff has just walked into the room with a plastic bag containing passionfruit, which had been brought from Brisbane a week or so before but been mislaid.

DI:	Did you find them?
GEOFF:	Passionfruit, yes.
DI:	What are they like?
JENNY:	Oh, beaut. (*Geoff laughs*)
DI:	What state are they in?
GEOFF:	Well, let's have a look at them.
JENNY:	They came from Brisbane, did they?
GEOFF:	Yes. Um . . . Yes, they must have fallen down behind the seat.

JENNY: Oh.

GEOFF: (*looking into the plastic bag*) Let's see what the situation is.

JENNY: Did they keep? Some of them keep fairly well.

GEOFF: Some of them don't.

JENNY: Some are OK.

GEOFF: They'll be all right inside.

JENNY: If they're cut open and I take the pulp out of them now, they'll probably . . . some of them'll probably be all right. I won't have the mouldy ones.

GEOFF: No.

We can consider the context of this spoken text under the same categories of field, tenor and mode as the written text:

Field   General: domestic arrangements. Specific: the provision of food (in particular, fruit) and the assessment of its condition. Although not explicit in the text, there is also the offering of a gift by people visiting the house.

Tenor   This is a conversation amongst three closely related adults, one male and two female. Geoff and Di are husband and wife, and Jenny is Geoff's sister; the social distance is minimal. The conversation takes place in Jenny's house, where Geoff and Di are visitors, but the host-guest relationship is overshadowed by the close family relationship.

Mode   Spoken language in a face-to-face situation. Speech continues while the passionfruit are brought in and examined: in other words, the topic of conversation is present (at first in a plastic bag). So the language is closely bound up with the action.

We see the speakers using language to identify bits of their world: *passionfruit, seat, pulp, the mouldy ones*. At the same time they represent what's been going on (*find, came, have fallen down*), states like *are* and *have* and other processes like *see* and *keep*. Then there are the circumstances in which these things have been or are going on: *from Brisbane, behind the seat, inside*.

This summary, together with the discussion of Text 1.1, gives a brief hint of the language resources available for representing our experience of the world (the *reflection* function of language), which will be explored further in the next chapter. In the remainder of this chapter we'll concentrate on aspects of the other two major language functions which we noted at the beginning: *action* and *connection*.

Acting upon the world

We act upon the world largely through interacting with other people. Certain parts of the grammar are available to serve this major function of language, which is usually referred to as the **interpersonal** function. It is associated with the tenor of the context. We can see how the grammar expresses such interpersonal meanings if we look more closely at two of the most basic kinds of interaction, namely:

- exchanging information (e.g. telling and asking)

- exchanging goods and services (e.g. offering and requesting).

In each of these activities we can both give and demand (or seek); these are roles in the exchange. When we combine them with the commodities being exchanged (information and goods and services), we can identify four main categories of meaning or speech functions, as this table shows:

Roles	Information	Goods and services
giving	statement	offer
demanding/seeking	question	command/request

In three of the four categories language is more or less essential, and there is a particular grammatical structure associated with each of them. The offer, however, does not have a distinctive grammatical structure of its own — it can be expressed in various ways. The grammatical structures which realise the other three functions are illustrated in the examples below, based on the passionfruit text. The terms shown beside each example refer to the grammatical structures themselves (i.e. to the way the words are arranged in the sentence), not to the functions they are normally used for.

statement (giving information)

    I have found the passionfruit.   *declarative*

question (seeking information)

    Have you found the passionfruit?   *interrogative*

command (demanding goods or services)

    Find the passionfruit.   *imperative*

The structures illustrated here (to which we shall return) are the most straightforward means of achieving these functions, but there are other possibilities. For instance, a question can be asked in this way:

        You've found the passionfruit?

Although this grammatical structure is normally used for a statement, it can function as a question if it is said with a question intonation (or written with a question mark). Thus intonation can override structure; its impact is more powerful. Young children often begin to ask questions in this way ('You find them?') before they've mastered the question structure.

Another possible structure for a question can be illustrated from Text 1.2; the answer is suggested but the question seeks confirmation:

> They came from Brisbane, did they?

On the other hand, the question structure is often used for requests seeking goods or services, as in this example (a request implicit in the context of Text 1.1):

> Would parents please sign and return the permission note?

As already mentioned, there is no special structure for the offer, which is not as common as the other functions. However, it can be achieved through a question structure, such as:

> Shall I cut the passionfruit open?
>
> Would you like me to cut the passionfruit open?

There is also the cooperative kind of offer, which has the same structure as a command:

> Let's have a look at them.

If we turn to the question itself and its own particular structure, the **interrogative**, we find that there are two very common types, each slightly different in function and structure. Compare these two examples:

> Did the passionfruit come from Brisbane?
>
> Where did the passionfruit come from?

The first can be answered by a simple *yes* or *no*; it's a question about the whole message, whether it is so or not. This type is termed a **yes/no question**. The second example is a question about a specific aspect of the message — in this case about place (*where?*). Similar questions could be formed with *who, what, when, how* and *why*, each probing a specific aspect of the message. Because most of these words begin with *wh-*, these questions are known as **WH questions**. The structure, which can serve other purposes besides seeking information, may be referred to as the **WH interrogative**. Examples of each type of question found in Text 1.2 are:

> **yes/no** Did you find them?
>
> They came from Brisbane, did they?
>
> Did they keep?
>
> **WH** What are they like?
>
> What state are they in?

We can summarise all these structures in a diagram. The choices they illustrate are described as choices of **mood**.

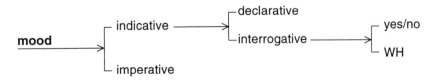

(The term *indicative* refers to the group of structures used in the exchange of information, whereas the *imperative* belongs to the exchange of goods and services.)

Each of these structures represents a different category of meaning and plays a different role in the exchange of meaning. We will explore them in more detail in Chapters 3 and 4.

Having the right connections

We use language for establishing connections both within the text we are producing and with the context in which we are operating. This is the third major function of language mentioned early in this chapter, and we will just glance at it here.

In Text 1.2, Di's opening question, *Did you find them?*, refers to something outside the text but in the context — namely, the passionfruit in the plastic bag which Geoff is carrying. (We can also assume that Geoff and Di had talked about these missing passionfruit before, so that the question also refers back to previous conversations.) In this conversation the passionfruit are referred to explicitly only once; every other reference is made with the words *they* and *them*, and it is this device which provides one of the links running through the text.

Related to it is another feature which helps to establish connections. As a text unfolds, some of the meanings involved can be taken for granted: the writer or speaker can present them as given and they can be contrasted with meanings that are new in the text. For example, in this exchange,

JENNY: Some of them keep fairly well.
GEOFF: Some of them don't.

there's no need for Geoff to repeat *keep fairly well*; that can be taken for granted. But later, when Jenny says *I won't have the mouldy ones*, only part of that is given: *ones* has been substituted for *passionfruit* but *mouldy* is new and so must be explicit and stressed in the way Jenny says it.

These are just some of the language features which make it obvious that we are dealing with a coherent text and not just a random collection of utterances. We will return to these features in Chapter 11.

Links with traditional grammar

In this chapter we have introduced some concepts that are well established in traditional grammar. For example, the notions of *statement*, *question* and *command* are well known as types of sentence. Even the terms *declarative*, *interrogative* and *imperative* are used in traditional grammar, though they may not be so generally familiar.

What is different in this grammar is that the starting point is the functions that language serves for us. As we've seen, one of the major functions is 'acting upon the world'. Within that broad function we can identify uses such as language for exchanging information and language for exchanging goods and services. Statement, question and command are traditional categories of meaning involved in these uses. Each has a typical grammatical structure by which they are often (but not always) expressed, as this table shows:

Use of language	Category of meaning	Grammatical structure
giving information	statement	declarative
seeking information	question	interrogative
demanding goods and services	command	imperative

Summary

The relationships between context and text and grammatical features which have been introduced in this chapter can be summarised thus:

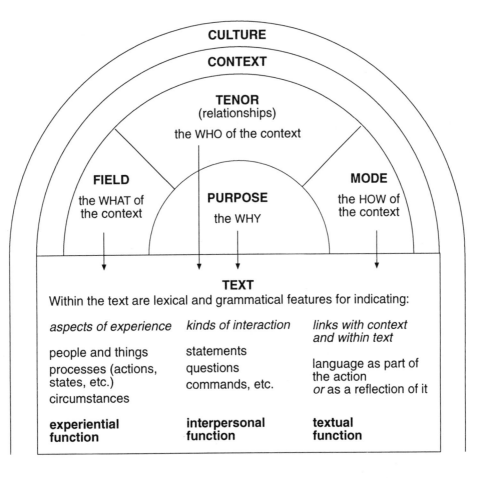

A Representation of the World

People often think of language as consisting of words. Traditional accounts of grammar usually start at the level of the word and discuss word classes such as nouns, verbs, adjectives, etc. — the so-called 'parts of speech'.

In this approach we focus on a different level of structure: namely, the **clause**. This is one of the most important structures in English grammar, for it is the one that carries a message. It allows us to bring several specific meanings together and show how they are related. It also allows us to show what part the message plays in interaction (statement, question, etc.) and how each message fits into the text and the context. Because most of our meaning is organised into clauses, we'll begin this chapter by considering the structure of the clause, looking at several examples from Text 2.1 before attempting a precise description.

TEXT 2.1 ADAPTED FROM A PAMPHLET ON CHEESE-MAKING AT BODALLA, NSW

Thomas Mort bought Bodalla, a cattle run on the Tuross River, from John Hawdon in 1856, and immediately began to form it into a model country estate. Land was cleared, swamps drained, dairy cattle imported and tenant farmers set up on different parts of the property. These tenant farmers made butter and cheese on their farms. The produce was bought by Mort and sold on the Sydney market. However, the farmers were poor cheese-makers and Mort was not satisfied with the quality, so he changed the system. He brought the dairy herds in to three main centres, where hundreds of cows were hand-milked on a contract basis. The milk was made into cheese in newly built factories by skilled cheese-makers brought out from England for this special task.

Most of the sentences in Text 2.1 have more than one clause. However, to begin with a simple example, here is a sentence which consists of only one clause:

> These tenant farmers made butter and cheese on their farms.

Now let's take a sentence which contains three clauses — three basic messages — shown here with one clause on each line:

> However, the farmers were poor cheese-makers
> and Mort was not satisfied with the quality,
> so he changed the system.

Each of these clauses begins with a conjunction (*However, and* and the informal *so*) to show their relationships within the sentence and with the preceding text.

Further possibilities are evident in two more sentences from the same text (again the clauses are shown line by line):

> Land was cleared,
> swamps drained,
> dairy cattle imported
> and tenant farmers set up on different parts of the property.

Here, only the last clause begins with a conjunction (*and*), and in the last three you have to supply the word *were*, derived from the *was* in the first clause.

> Thomas Mort bought Bodalla, a cattle run on the Tuross River, from John Hawdon in 1856,
> and immediately began to form it into a model country estate.

In this case, the first clause (running on to a second line) includes an explanation of what Bodalla was, but that is all part of the one clause.

So what is a clause?

We can describe the clause as a structure in which several components of meaning are brought together to form a message. The message is normally based on a process — that is, an action or state of affairs through which the other components are related. Any clause can exist as an independent sentence or it can be incorporated into a longer sentence, usually with the addition of some linking word. Correspondingly, a **sentence** consists of a single clause or two or more clauses linked together.

The clause can be seen as a representation of some aspect of our experience, and as such it serves the **experiential** function of language. This is what we described in Chapter 1 as language for reflecting our experience of the world. It is also known as the **ideational** function.

In any clause we can identify certain components of experience which are represented by particular structures (a word or a group of words). Each component has a particular function in the clause. Returning to our first example from Text 2.1, we can identify these components:

These tenant farmers	made	butter and cheese	on their farms.
participant	process	participant	circumstance

To make sure that these components are meaningful units in the clause (and not just arbitrary groups of words), we can try recasting the clause in different ways:

On their farms	these tenant farmers	made	butter and cheese.

Butter and cheese	were made	on their farms	by these tenant farmers.

The functions of the components within the clause can be further illustrated by posing some questions about a shorter but comparable clause: *The farmers made cheese on their farms.* Note that in all but the first of the questions the process component is changed and split up — that's a requirement of the question structure.

Who made cheese on the farms?	The farmers.
What did the farmers make on their farms?	Cheese.
Where did the farmers make the cheese?	On their farms.
What did the farmers do on their farms?	Made cheese.

The answer to the last question requires two components (*made* and *cheese*), which shows that there is a very close link between them.

More about components

There are three main kinds of components in the clause: **participants, processes** and **circumstances**. Each represents a different aspect of experience:

participants: refer to the 'things' in our experience ('things' in this sense including people)

processes: indicate what's going on, or the state of affairs

circumstances: describe features of the context in which the processes take place (e.g. the time, the place, the manner).

Much of our experience is conceived in terms of 'things' and happenings. The clause is usually built around the happenings — processes of doing, feeling, being and so on — and it's possible to have clauses which consist only of a process, such as:

Stop!   Don't jump!   It's raining.

In the last example, however, *It* is a kind of dummy participant, and even the first two can be said to imply a participant, *you*, as the following extension reveals:

> Don't jump, will you!

Certainly it's more usual to have at least one participant explicit, as in the following examples (where the process component is shown in italics):

> The jug's *boiling.*   Rufus *leapt.*
>
> The house *was painted.*   Part of the freeway *collapsed.*

One of the sentences from Text 2.1 provides further examples:

> Land *was cleared,* swamps *(were) drained,* dairy cattle *(were) imported* ...

In the next group of examples there are two participants. Each clause begins and ends with a participant; the process (in italics) shows the relationship between them.

> The koala *may be* an endangered species.
>
> Restaurants *should stop selling* frogs' legs.
>
> They *are redecorating* their house.
>
> The robber captain *said* the magic words.

It's even possible to have three participants in the one clause, though this is unusual except where the process is one of giving or providing:

My aunt	gave	him	the rowing boat.
participant	process	participant	participant

He	made	the children	a swing.
participant	process	participant	participant

Many clauses include a circumstance, especially one of time or place. In the next group of examples the circumstance is the last component, after the italicised process:

> The town *was established* in 1842.   They *came* from Brisbane.
>
> Low tide *is* at 5.03 a.m.   Money *doesn't grow* on trees.

In the next two examples the components are in a different order:

Great oaks	from little acorns	grow.
participant	circumstance	process

Into the valley of Death	rode	the six hundred.
circumstance	process	participant

We'll now look more closely at the three main components of the clause (*participants, processes* and *circumstances*), as they are some of the most important resources our language offers us for making sense of the world and for representing our experience.

Participants: what we're on about

Our language offers us ways of referring to all the 'things' in our world — though, as mentioned earlier, 'things' in this sense has to be taken pretty broadly. It includes people, objects, places and abstract concepts, which are all 'things' that can be talked about. We've already seen some examples in Chapter 1, and here are some more from a spread of contexts:

chocolates	steel
Churchill	Grandma Moses
the traffic lights	a red light
Brisbane	the Brisbane River
highly toxic gases	a fly in the ointment
a load of concrete	a load of codswallop
the black stump	the third street on the left
life after death	belief in life after death
the Royal Australian Navy	people who live in glass houses
a car driving on the wrong side of the road	the busiest airport in the southern hemisphere

As you can see, there's quite a variety. While some are single words, most are groups of words. But even the groups vary: some are short and simple, some quite long. However, they all have one thing in common: they all include a word of a particular type — namely, a **noun**. Each of these examples is based on a key noun and all of them, even the single words, can be referred to as **noun groups** (a structure explained more fully in Chapter 6).

It is noun groups like these which function as participants in clauses. We use them for referring to the 'things' in the world, and we can refer to virtually any thing by means of a noun group. For some things there is a precise word and so the noun group may be as simple as:

rubber	Napoleon	books
the council	a spanner	an apple

Here the noun group consists of just a single noun, or a noun preceded by *the* or *a* (or *an*).

Often, however, there's no single word that means the exact thing we want to refer to, and so we build up a more complex noun group to identify clearly the thing we mean and to distinguish it from other similar things. Here are some examples:

the cake which her aunt made for her birthday

King George VI

green bananas

the house on the right just past the bridge

children coming home from school

Pronouns

There's another way of referring to the 'things' in our experience — there are some words in the language which function like noun groups although they don't look like them. They are the words like *he*, *she*, *it* and *they* (and their related forms *his*, *him*, *her*, etc.). They are known as **pronouns** and, specifically, as **reference pronouns**. They are in fact a special kind of noun group which can take the place of other noun groups, and they are used extensively for referring to things. However, they can only be used when the thing has already been identified in the text (or is about to be identified), or when they refer to something that is obvious in the context in which the language is being used. We will have more to say about them in Chapter 3.

Processes: what's going on

We don't usually just talk about 'things' in isolation; we say what's going on or what state of affairs exists. Things are related to each other; people do things and have feelings; things happen. So, in representing our experience, we also refer to these processes: actions, mental states, relationships and so on. The words and structures for doing this are a second kind of experiential resource, another kind of clause component.

There are of course occasions when we might refer to things without indicating any process: for example, in taking notes, or in labels or book titles, but these are special cases where the context indicates the state of affairs or whatever process applies.

Here are some examples in which the italicised words indicate the processes:

Charity *begins* at home. She *loves* me; she *loves* me not.

The children *will be visiting* Taronga. I *know* about it already.

The old pub *has been pulled* down. We'*ll think* of something.

Ambrose *cooked* the dinner. The driver *couldn't see* a thing.

The dinner *was cooking*.

What *did* you *say*? This *is* the Woodville Road.

He *whispered* the answer to him. What state *are* they in?

'*Look out!*' she *yelled*. Where'*s* the soap?

He *seems* the best person for the job.

The italicised words and groups of words expressing the process in these examples illustrate the structure known as the **verb group**. They are all based on one type of word: namely, the **verb**. Often the verb group consists of just one word — the verb itself — or even just a part of a word (such as '*s* for *is* or *has*). However, the verb group is often a group of two or more words which are so closely related that the whole group is sometimes referred to simply as 'the verb', especially in traditional grammar.

Verbs are a class of words which we can identify by certain formal features (e.g. they can have an -*ing* ending added). These features will be discussed in Chapter 8. The kind of meaning verbs have is referred to as a process — that is, verbs provide us with a means of indicating what is happening or what state of affairs exists.

When the verb group consists of more than one word, it usually begins with a member of a small class of words closely related to the verb. They are known as **auxiliaries** (or **auxiliary verbs**) and they contribute certain special meanings to the process that the verb is expressing. A few of them can be used either as auxiliaries or as verbs in their own right; these include *be, have* and *do* and their related forms.

The structure of the verb groups in the first two examples above can be shown as follows:

begins		will be	visiting
verb		auxiliaries	verb
verb group		verb group	

What are the circumstances?

So far we've surveyed the resources which our language offers for referring to the 'things' in our experience and for indicating the processes which relate them. The third aspect of experience which can be readily expressed in language is the circumstances in which the processes are going on. For example, we often want to indicate when and where something happened or how it happened, or when and where some state of affairs existed. Such circumstances of time, place and manner are the commonest ones, though there are several others.

English is fairly well supplied with words, phrases and other structures by which all these circumstances can be expressed. In the following examples the word or other structure indicating the circumstance is italicised:

I start my new job *tomorrow.*

Once upon a time there were three bears.

Thomas Mort bought Bodalla *in 1856.*

Put it *there.*

The passionfruit came *from Brisbane.*

Down a sunny dirt road, over a log bridge, up a grassy hill, deep in Bear Country, lived a family of bears.

She performed the operation *very skilfully.*

We'll have a drink *for old times' sake.*

The fete was postponed *because of the rain.*

There is much variety in the way the circumstances can be expressed — for instance:

- a single word (*tomorrow, there*)
- a small group of words (*from Brisbane, very skilfully*)
- a larger group of words (*because of the rain*).

It's also possible to express circumstances by means of a clause — for example, a clause of time or reason, related to another clause by some linking word like *when* or *because*. These words and structures will discussed more fully in Chapter 8.

The circumstance of time

The notion of time is a special case. Not only can it be expressed as a circumstance within a clause or through a clause of its own — it can also be indicated (very broadly) by changes made to the verb group. There is a basic distinction between past time and non-past which is marked by a variation in the form of the verb:

> The plane took off for Singapore at 1715.
> The plane takes off for Singapore at 1715.
>
> The house was being painted in garish colours.
> The house is being painted in garish colours.
>
> Everyone loved her.
> Everyone loves her.

There are other time-related implications that verbs and verb groups can have (to be discussed in Chapter 8), but the more specific and subtle circumstances of time have to be expressed by the kind of adverbial structures outlined above.

Building up the picture

In this chapter we've been looking at how the clause serves the experiential function of language, enabling us to represent and make sense of our experience of the world. We have identified:

- ways of referring to the 'things' in the world (*participants*)
- ways of indicating what's going on (*processes*)
- ways of indicating features of the context (*circumstances*).

We build up our picture of the world by putting these resources together in the structure of the clause. They function as components of the clause. However, a clause is not simply a collection of components. The crucial thing is the way the components are related to each other through the process. This is called the **transitivity** relationship, and it will be explored more fully in Chapter 5.

Yet though a clause has this experiential function in language, it's usually playing an interpersonal role at the same time. For example, when we're interacting with other people by making a statement or asking a question, we generally have some process (something happening, some state of affairs) and some 'things' (people, places, objects, concepts and so on) participating in the process. There may also be a mention of the circumstances in which the process takes place. It is through the clause, with its three kinds of component, that we can present each part of our picture of the world.

Summary and a note on links with traditional grammar

The main concept introduced in this chapter is the *clause* — a concept quite well established in traditional grammar. However, while there's not much difference in what would be identified as clauses in the two approaches, we should note the following points:

1 Traditional grammar does not deal with the function of the clause in the way this approach does.

2 Traditional grammar does not deal with the structure of the clause in terms of the main components described in this chapter. None the less these components can each be related to one of the traditional parts of speech (i.e. word classes):

component	structure	based on
participant	noun group	noun
process	verb group	verb
circumstance	several possible structures	adverb or adverbial phrase

Language for Interaction

In Chapter 2 we were concerned with the grammar of the *experiential* function of language — the resources we have for representing our experience and making sense of the world. In this and the next chapter we return to another major function of language introduced in Chapter 1: namely, the *interpersonal* function, or language for acting upon the world. The effect of both these major language functions can be seen in the grammatical structure of any clause, since we draw upon our experience as we operate on the world.

We constantly use language to make our way in the world, interacting with other people and getting on with the business and pleasures of life. Acting upon the world usually means acting on or in conjunction with other people, especially in the give-and-take of interaction. This can be seen most obviously in face-to-face conversation, but it applies in principle to other speech situations, and to communication through the written word and other media as well.

As we make our way in the world, we use language for a number of specific purposes. One group of these purposes, introduced in Chapter 1, revolves around the giving and seeking of information — what's called the **information exchange**. In this chapter we will explore the grammar of the information exchange more fully, and then in the next chapter we will consider some further aspects of the interpersonal function.

Exchanging information

As we saw in Chapter 1, the exchange of information principally involves making statements and asking questions. There is a particular grammatical structure typically used for a clause making a statement (the *declarative*) and another typically used for asking questions (the *interrogative*). If we consider some pairs of examples, we can identify the main grammatical features of the two structures:

It is raining in Sydney.
Is it raining in Sydney?

We will be trapped.
Will we be trapped?

They have been renting a holiday flat on the north coast.
Have they been renting a holiday flat on the north coast?

If we compare the interrogative form with the declarative in these pairs of examples, we can see that certain words have been rearranged. Yet, strictly speaking, it's not so much words that are rearranged as certain components, and we need to identify them in order to specify what's happening.

If we used the terms introduced in the last chapter, we would describe the components of one of these examples as follows:

They	have been renting	a holiday flat	on the north coast.
participant	process	participant	circumstance
noun group	*verb group*	*noun group*	*phrase*

However, these functional components (participant, process, circumstance) are aspects of experience. In order to describe the clause's interpersonal function, we need to identify different components.

The component which plays the most crucial role in the switch from declarative to interrogative (and in other interpersonal meanings) is known as the **mood**. In Chapter 1 we used the term *mood* to refer to the system of choices involved; here, however, it is used to refer to the clause component through which the choice is indicated. This mood component consists of two elements, the **subject** and the **finite**, each of which requires some explanation.

In a declarative clause, the subject is normally the first participant, the one which precedes the verb group. There are several ways of testing for the subject. The traditional test is to pose a question by asking *who* or *what* with the verb group (e.g. *Who or what has been renting a flat . . . ?*); the answer is the subject (i.e. *they*). Another test is to see which participant comes into a 'tag' (a term to be explained later in this chapter — it refers to *have they?* in the following example):

They have been renting a holiday flat, have they?

The role of the finite element is to limit the scope of the verb in its time reference or its degree of certainty. In all the examples used so far in this chapter, the finite is the *first auxiliary* in the verb group (e.g. it's the *will* in *will be trapped*, where it denotes futurity).

The example below shows the mood component and its two important elements, the subject and the finite. The rest of the clause, known as the **residue**, is not analysed.

They	have	been renting a holiday flat on the north coast.
subject	finite	
mood		residue

Forming the interrogative — the basic rule

The essential feature of the interrogative structure is that the subject *follows* the finite. So, to form an interrogative from a declarative, move the finite element so that it comes *before* the subject. The rest of the clause remains unchanged.

Have	they	been renting a holiday flat on the north coast?
finite	subject	
mood		residue

However, the finite element does not necessarily move to the beginning of the clause; it simply changes places with the subject, as the following example shows:

> By the way, it's raining in Sydney.
> By the way, is it raining in Sydney?

Even if there's a very long subject, it's still possible to form an interrogative by applying the basic rule — the finite comes before the subject:

> Anyone who wants to come and help with the supper can see the show for nothing.
> Can anyone who wants to come and help with the supper see the show for nothing?

The same applies in this WH interrogative from a 5-year-old girl who was colouring in:

> What colour can a windmill's thing that turns around be?

What if there's no auxiliary?

Where is the finite in these declarative clauses?

> Jenny saw the emu beside the road.   It often rains in Sydney.
>
> One good turn deserves another.   Geoff found the passionfruit.

The answer may at first seem a little puzzling — there's no finite visible. The reason is that in these examples the finite element is fused with the verb (i.e. there's no first auxiliary) and the verb group consists simply of the verb by itself. To form interrogatives from these clauses, it's necessary to bring in a dummy auxiliary so that we can separate the finite from the verb. For this purpose there's a stand-by verb, *do* (including its parts *does*, *did*, *doing* and *done*), and we operate as if the declarative clause had the form, *Jenny did see the emu beside the road*. The added auxiliary *did* carries the finite element (which means that it marks the tense) and so the main verb reverts to its basic form (*saw* becomes *see*). Now the interrogatives can be formed according to the basic rule:

Did Jenny see the emu beside the road?   Does it often rain in Sydney?

Does one good turn deserve another?   Did Geoff find the passionfruit?

The special group: be and have

There are two verbs that don't make such a fuss about forming interrogatives: *be* (*am, is, are*, etc.) and *have* (*has, had*). Both can operate as auxiliaries themselves on occasions. *Be* is the simplest case; *have* is a bit more problematical. Let's look at *be* first:

She's a good singer.
Is she a good singer?

You are being honest with yourself.
Are you being honest with yourself?

In the first pair of examples there's no auxiliary (the finite element being fused with the main verb) and the subject simply changes place with the verb to form the interrogative. The fact that *be* can operate as an auxiliary on occasions perhaps makes it easier to accept this way of forming the interrogative. In the second pair of examples both the auxiliary and the verb are forms of *be*. The auxiliary is the finite element and the interrogative is formed in the usual way: the finite comes before the subject.

Have can form interrogatives in several ways. We'll look at some examples based on the declarative clause, *You have a watch*. There are at least three possible forms of interrogative:

Have you a watch?

Have you got a watch?

Do you have a watch?

The first option follows the same pattern as *be*: the verb itself comes before the subject. This form isn't common in Australian English but it is possible. The second option exploits the similarity in meaning between these two clauses:

You have a watch.   You've got a watch.

The *have* in the first clause is treated as an auxiliary in the second, with *get* as the verb, and thus the interrogative can be formed in the usual way (finite before subject). The third option (*Do you have a watch?*) is the normal form for verbs without an auxiliary: the stand-by auxiliary *do* is brought in to be the finite element. This is the normal interrogative for *have* in American English, and it's also widely used in Australia — as is the second form, *Have you got a watch?*

WH interrogatives

The examples we've been discussing so far are all of the *yes/no* type of interrogative, used when the whole message of the clause is in question. However, you will recall from Chapter 1 a second type, the WH interrogative, used when only one particular part of the message is in question. Generally in such clauses one participant is (or includes) a WH word. Consider the following examples, based on the clause, *Jenny saw the emu beside the road*.

> Who saw the emu beside the road?
>
> What did Jenny see beside the road?
>
> Where did Jenny see the emu?

Each of these examples focuses on one component of the original declarative clause, for only one piece of information is being sought. Where the first participant (the subject) is in question, as in the first example, the word order of the rest of the clause is not affected:

> Jenny ⎫
>   ⎬ saw the emu beside the road(?)
> Who   ⎭

But since the WH component normally comes at the beginning of the clause, there are changes to other components in the other two WH questions (*What . . . ?* and *Where . . . ?*). These changes are the same as in a *yes/no* interrogative: the finite comes before the subject. In the examples above, because the original verb group *saw* hasn't got an auxiliary (the finite being fused with the main verb), the stand-by auxiliary *did* (from *do*) is brought in.

There is another type of question, the **alternative** question, which in some respects is like a *yes/no* question. The classic example is:

> Do you want tea or coffee?

Speech role pronouns

In the last section we compared a number of clause pairs in which one clause was a declarative and the other its interrogative equivalent. However, while the idea of changing a declarative into its interrogative form is useful for illustrating the grammatical relationships, it is rather artificial when we consider the way the clauses might occur in real human interaction. We can get a bit closer to the realities of dialogue if we put the interrogative first to produce a question-and-answer sequence. But then we also have to change from *you* to *I* as we go from interrogative to declarative:

> Have you got a watch?
> I've got a watch.

Of course the answer's still rather artificial because we'd probably just say *yes* or *no*. We don't normally answer in a 'full sentence' — but that's another story, to which we'll return in Chapter 12. Nevertheless this pair of clauses does illustrate one simple yet basic aspect of the use of language for interacting with other people: namely, that our language enables us to cast ourselves in the role of speaker and others in the role of addressee(s), the person or people we are addressing. We do this with the simple words *I* and *you* (together with their related forms *me*, *my*, *mine* and *your*, *yours*).

These words are known as **pronouns** and, specifically, as **speech role pronouns**. They contrast with the *reference pronouns* introduced in the previous chapter, which are further discussed in Chapter 6.

You is not quite as simple as *I* because it may refer either to a single listener or to a group. In present-day standard English we have no simple way of distinguishing between these two meanings of *you* (the singular and the plural), though most of the time there's no difficulty because the context makes it obvious. When it doesn't, we can resort to naming the person we are addressing or to using a phrase like 'all of you'. However, in non-standard Australian English the distinction can be made more simply: if more than one person is being addressed, the word *youse* is available (the unstressed form is sometimes written *yez*).

Another speech role pronoun is *we* (with *us*, *our* and *ours*). In using this pronoun the speaker identifies himself or herself with at least one other person. The meaning of *we* always includes the speaker, but who else it includes can vary according to the context. These are the main possibilities:

inclusive *we*: speaker + addressee(s) ('you and I').

exclusive *we*: speaker + someone/people other than the addressee(s) ('he/she/they and I').

In a written text like this book, the authorial *we* (writer + readers) is an inclusive *we* through which a writer seeks to include the readers in the discourse. Another inclusive use is the generalised *we* ('you and I and everyone'), where the speaker speaks on behalf of people in general.

Perhaps the most exclusive *we* is the so-called royal *we*, which has come to mean 'I, with superior status'. It's just one instance of the way these speech role pronouns can get caught up in the power play of interpersonal relationships.

In English we just have the one word *we* for all these meanings, though that's rarely a problem because the context usually makes the meaning clear. However, in some languages (including some Australian Aboriginal languages and some in Papua New Guinea) there are different words for inclusive *we* and exclusive *we*.

A departure from tradition

Traditionally these speech role pronouns are known as *personal pronouns* and the roles of speaker and addressee are described as:

1st person	(person speaking)	I	we
2nd person	(person spoken to)	you	

The reference pronouns mentioned in Chapter 2 are also traditionally classed as personal pronouns, and they are described as:

| 3rd person | ('person' spoken about) | he | she | it |
| | | they | | |

Here the term 'person' has to be taken not in its general sense but as a grammatical term which includes *it* as well as actual persons.

It must be admitted that in some ways it's convenient to group all these 'personal' pronouns together as one class of word, as traditional grammar does. But it's also important to recognise a significant difference in their use: the speech role pronouns (first and second person) indicate the roles people are playing in the interaction, while the reference pronouns (third person) form part of the subject matter of the discourse.

The exchange of speech roles and the shift to a reference pronoun are neatly caught in this fragment of dialogue from 'The Goon Show'. The Goons think they have found some lost people in a mine shaft and one of them is shouting down the shaft:

GOON:	Are you all right?
(ECHO):	Are you all right?
GOON:	We're all right!
(ECHO):	We're all right!
GOON:	(*to the others*) Whew! Thank goodness they're all right.

The fact that the pronouns *I* and *you* represent speech roles can also be seen in the difficulty young children may experience in working out that *you* is not a name for themselves but a role they play temporarily. Some young children say things like, 'You want one', when they actually mean, 'I want one'.

Negative grammar

In the examples discussed so far in this chapter there are no negatives. Yet we often want to refer to what's not happening in the world as well as what's happening, or to identify a state of affairs that doesn't exist as well as one that does. So our grammatical system has positive and negative poles, just as magnets and electrical systems do. Whether a clause is negative or positive can be described as its **polarity**, and we must now explore how the negative option operates.

Forming negatives — the basic rule

The basic rule is simple: insert *not* after the finite. Compare these two pairs of examples:

| It is raining in Sydney. | The land has been sold to a developer. |
| It is not raining in Sydney. | The land has not been sold to a developer. |

In the negative clauses of each pair, the word *not* has been inserted straight after the finite element — the first auxiliary (i.e. *is* and *has*) — illustrating the basic rule for making a positive clause negative.

However, we can also put these things slightly differently:

It's raining in Sydney.   The land's been sold to a developer.

In these versions the first auxiliary has been contracted with the subject. We began with the uncontracted forms because in them the negative rule can be seen operating more clearly. But contractions are more usual in informal usage, and in the negative versions the *not* contracts with the first auxiliary (now uncontracted), so that we get:

It isn't raining in Sydney.   The land hasn't been sold to a developer.

In effect the *not* becomes part of the finite, limiting the scope of the verb. Another possibility, which puts more emphasis on the negative, is:

It's not raining in Sydney.   The land's not been sold to a developer.

The basic rule for forming negatives, then, is like that for interrogatives and involves the first auxiliary, whether it's contracted or not.

What if there's no auxiliary?

Once again, if the finite is fused with the main verb, the stand-by verb *do* is used whenever we need an auxiliary to carry the finite. Consider these groups of examples:

Jenny saw the emu beside the road.
Jenny did not see the emu beside the road.
Jenny didn't see the emu beside the road.

One good turn deserves another.
One good turn does not deserve another.
One good turn doesn't deserve another.

It often rains in Sydney.
It does not often rain in Sydney
It doesn't often rain in Sydney.
It doesn't rain very often in Sydney.

In each of the negative clauses the *not* has been inserted after the finite auxiliary, which is a form of the verb *do* brought in specially for the occasion. Like other auxiliaries, these often form a contraction with the *not*, which is tacked on as -*n't* (e.g. *doesn't*).

In the last set of examples, however, the positive form already has a word between the subject *it* and the verb group *rains*. The word *often* represents a circumstance of time/frequency. This doesn't affect the negative rule; *not* comes in after the first auxiliary as usual. But in the negative form of this particular example it's quite likely that the *often* would follow the verb group and be modified in some way — hence the last version, *It doesn't rain very often in Sydney.*

The special group: be and have

These verbs do things a bit differently if they have no auxiliary. In the case of *be*, the *not* is simply put in after the verb — and it may or may not be contracted:

> She's a good singer.
> She isn't a good singer.
> She's not a good singer.

When we make *have* negative, we usually bring in an alternative main verb and treat the *have* as an auxiliary, just as we can in forming *have* interrogatives. So the *not* comes in after the first auxiliary after all:

> I have a watch.   *or*   I've got a watch.
> I haven't got a watch.

It's also possible to say:

> I haven't a watch.
> I've not got a watch.
> I don't have a watch.

These possibilities all allow for different kinds of emphasis, but the only two which are really common in Australian English are:

> I haven't got a watch.   *(have's idiosyncratic negative)*
> I don't have a watch.   *(the basic rule + stand-by do)*

Negative interrogatives

We've seen that the rules for forming interrogatives and negatives are similar in that both involve a finite auxiliary and both require the stand-by verb *do* if there's no auxiliary in the basic clause. It's also possible to have negative interrogatives. They may sound like a mouthful but they are something we often use, as these examples should indicate:

> Aren't you going to the dinner?   Doesn't it often rain in Sydney?
> Are you not going to the dinner?
>   Isn't she a good singer?
> Won't we be trapped?   Is she not a good singer?

As we know, the finite auxiliary comes before the subject to form the interrogative. If the *not* is contracted with the auxiliary, it also precedes the subject; otherwise it comes after the subject but before the rest of the verb group. The last example with *is* (a form of *be*) goes its own way.

Negative WH interrogatives are quite possible too, and the same principles apply, as these examples show:

> Why didn't I get one?   Why did I not get one?

Other negatives

There are other ways in which the negative idea can be expressed besides using *not*, and we will glance at some of them here. To begin with, there are some words with negative forms that carry the negative meaning and remove the need for *not*. Examples are:

> nobody   neither . . . nor   never

The negative can also be expressed as a quantity, as in:

> We have no eggs.   There's no milk left.

and special expressions like 'zero population growth'.

In addition, there are some pairs of opposites in which one word can be seen as the negative of the other:

> go/stop   hard/soft
>
> live/die   hot/cold

Emphatic clauses

There are times in the course of interaction when we want to give a clause special emphasis. This sometimes happens when an earlier statement has been challenged. For example, in Text 1.2, Geoff says of the passionfruit:

> They'll be all right inside.

But if Jenny had expressed more doubt about their condition, Geoff might have insisted:

> They *will* be all right inside.

Another example, illustrating both possibilities, comes from an interview on TV:

> We didn't know, that's what I'm saying, we just *did not* know.

The basic rule is to put the main stress on the first auxiliary (though sometimes a negative like *not* will take an equal or heavier stress). Often this is only evident in speech, but even so, as the examples above show, an otherwise contracted auxiliary (-*'ll*) or negative (-*n't*) must be uncontracted (*will*, *not*). Contraction implies lack of stress.

And if there is no auxiliary? Just bring in *do*. For example, if you were accused of leaving some gates open, you might say:

> I *did* shut the gates.   (*cf.* I shut the gates.)

Getting things tagged

One aspect of the exchange of information that's very common in everyday conversation has not yet been discussed. This is the **tag question**, often referred to simply as the **tag**. A way of seeking confirmation for something more or less expected, it modifies the impact of straight declaratives and interrogatives and so helps the dialogue to run more smoothly. Compare the implications of these two questions:

> Did you shut the gates?
> You shut the gates, didn't you?

While the first simply seeks information, the second seeks confirmation of something the speaker hopes is true. It reveals the speaker's expectations; it is based on shared knowledge and a degree of understanding between speaker and addressee.

The tag question is very much a device of conversation rather than writing. It's very common in friendly, informal conversation amongst people who are close to each other. In these circumstances, people often seek confirmation rather than information because they can to some degree anticipate what will pass between them — it's an indication of how closely in touch with each other they are.

A tag can follow a positive or a negative clause, each perhaps with slightly different implications, though this will vary with the context:

> The gates are all shut, aren't they?
> You didn't leave any gates open, did you?

The speaker may be more or less certain about the information in question, and this can be conveyed by the way in which these tagged clauses are said — the kind of intonation pattern they're given. The basic choice is between a rising tone and a falling tone on the tag. A falling tone implies more certainty than a rising one. We can only hint at this in conventional writing by omitting the question mark for the falling tone:

> The gates are all shut, aren't they?
> The gates are all shut, aren't they.

There are other ways of varying the structure that don't depend purely on intonation. Compare these examples:

> You shut the gates, didn't you?
> You did shut the gates, didn't you?
> You shut the gates, did you?

While the first two both imply that the speaker expects the gates to be shut, the second (with its emphatic *did*) suggests that the need for confirmation is greater. By contrast, the last implies some surprise on the speaker's part that the gates have been shut at all.

Some ways of using the tag question vary in different regional dialects of English, but the types most common in Australian English have been illustrated here. There are other ways of seeking confirmation too — though it's rarely necessary to do so in such an explicit and formal way as this:

> Can you confirm that all the gates are shut?

The grammar of the tag

In the most typical uses of the tag question, the tag and the clause it follows are related to each other in regular ways. The basic clause is declarative, while the tag is interrogative and works in the same way as other interrogatives do (i.e. the subject follows the finite element). If the tag is negative, the *not* (or *-n't*) follows the finite. If the verb in the basic clause has no auxiliary, a form of *do* stands in for one. If the basic clause is positive, the tag is usually negative and vice versa. For example:

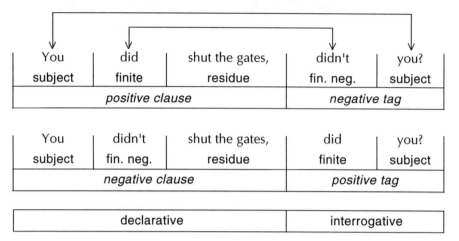

You	did	shut the gates,	didn't	you?
subject	finite	residue	fin. neg.	subject
positive clause			*negative tag*	

You	didn't	shut the gates,	did	you?
subject	fin. neg.	residue	finite	subject
negative clause			*positive tag*	

declarative	interrogative

If the subject of the basic clause is a noun group other than a simple pronoun, then a pronoun takes its place in the tag:

> The gates are all shut, aren't they.
>
> Uncle David didn't leave the gates open, did he?

It is always the subject of the basic clause which is picked up in the tag, even if via a reference pronoun. So, as we remarked earlier, applying a tag to a clause is one of the ways of checking what the subject is.

Conclusion and links with traditional grammar

Much of the grammar described in this chapter deals with structures we use continually without thinking in everyday conversation. Yet, when we examine them, we can see how regular and rule-governed they are. This applies especially to the way the subject and finite are used and what happens to the finite when there's no auxiliary.

Most of the general concepts, such as questions and negatives, are familiar from traditional grammar. However, the details are different. The basic rules involving the finite and the first auxiliary are not presented in these terms in traditional grammar; nor is the distinction between *yes/no* questions and WH questions. Furthermore, while traditional grammar pays a good deal of attention to personal pronouns, it does not make the important distinction between the speech role pronouns (traditional first and second person) and the reference pronouns (traditional third person), which takes account of the different functions these two groups of pronouns have in the language.

Another feature that's usually ignored in traditional grammar is the tag. This is because its most obvious role is in conversation, and traditional grammar deals almost exclusively with written English.

CHAPTER
4

Negotiating and Directing

One evening a visiting couple arrived at our front door. At the same time our cat arrived, carrying in its mouth our neighbours' pet budgerigar. One of our guests observed, ever so politely: 'I think your cat has something in its mouth.' She put it this way not because it was merely her opinion — the cat quite clearly had a bird in its mouth — but because she wanted to draw our attention to the awkwardness gently, without appearing to accuse us of having an uncontrolled cat. Opening with 'I think . . .' was a way of toning down the bluntness of: 'Your cat has something in its mouth!'

In interacting with other people, there are times when we do use very simple and blunt language. Equally, however, as was the case with the budgerigar, there are times when we want to modify our language. It may be because we are uncertain of our information, but more often than not it's because we want to be friendly, polite, sensitive, diplomatic, subtle, or even devious. Although we want to get things done, we also want to get on with people.

The ways in which we can modify our language for these purposes include the grammatical devices of **modality** and **modulation**, which will be dealt with in this chapter. They are, self-evidently, features of the interpersonal function of language — our resources for interacting with others and making our way in the world. We'll begin by considering the role of modality in the exchange of information and then go on to the ways in which we demand or seek goods and services — i.e. ways in which we get people to do things.

Modality: how certain can you be?

When we are exchanging information, we are sometimes quite certain about the matter involved. Our answer to a straightforward question, such as, *Is that the neighbours' budgerigar?*, may be a straightforward *yes* or *no* — positive or negative. The same certainty can apply to WH interrogatives:

What bird is that?
{
That is the neighbours' budgerigar.
    or
That is not the neighbours' budgerigar.
}

However, between these extremes of certainty there are many gradations; we don't always provide information with absolute conviction. There are other possible answers to the question, *Is that the neighbours' budgerigar?*, such as:

Maybe.	I think so.
Perhaps.	I doubt it.
Probably.	

In the same context other statements are possible too:

That could be the neighbours' budgerigar.	
That may be . . .	That seems to be . . .
That must be . . .	Perhaps that's . . .
That's probably . . .	I think that's . . .
It's likely that's the neighbours' budgerigar.	

Slightly more colloquial possibilities include:

I guess that's . . .	I reckon that's . . .
That would have to be the neighbours' budgerigar.	

Although these are almost all positive statements, none of them expresses absolute certainty. What they do express is varying degrees of certainty or uncertainty about whether it is the neighbours' budgerigar. They also illustrate several different grammatical resources for expressing degrees of certainty. This is the feature of the grammar known as *modality*.

The grammar of modality

We'll now consider some of these resources in more detail, beginning with an example from Text 1.2, where Geoff and Jenny are speculating about the passionfruit:

GEOFF: They'll be all right inside.
JENNY: If they're cut open and I take the pulp out of them now, they'll probably . . . some of them'll probably be all right. I won't have the mouldy ones.

The essence of Jenny's speculation is *some of them'll probably be all right*, where *probably* has been inserted into the verb group immediately after the first auxiliary -'*ll* (i.e. *will*). There are several other words that could be used in the same way, such as *possibly*, *certainly* and *undoubtedly*. In this position the modality is closely integrated into the clause. But such words can also occupy other positions, where they tend to bring the modality into sharper focus:

> Probably some of them'll be all right.

> Some of them'll be all right, most probably.

In addition, words like *possibly*, *probably* and *certainly* can be included (with a change of form) in an introductory clause:

> It's possible that some of them'll be all right.

> It's probable that . . .   It's almost certain that . . .

A speaker can also express a view on the subject matter in this way:

> I think . . .   I'm almost certain that . . .

> I believe . . .   I have no doubt that . . .

Furthermore, the various grammatical resources available for this kind of meaning can be used in combination — for example:

> I think the bird is probably dead.

> I surmise that it's possible that the historically Caucasian groups arose from a hybridisation between African and Asiatic peoples.

> > (from a radio talk)

The modal auxiliaries

The most basic way in which modality can be expressed is by a modification to the verb group itself. There is a group of words called **modal auxiliaries**, or simply **modals**, which can express these meanings. We've already encountered modals in the examples given above, including *may*, *could* and *must*. Text 1.2 provides two typical examples:

> They must have fallen down behind the seat.

> They'll be all right inside.

Modal auxiliaries fit into the verb group much like any other auxiliary. They are always placed first, before other auxiliaries (e.g. *must have fallen*), and that means that they always carry the finite element. The main modal auxiliaries are these:

can	shall	will	may	must	ought to
could	should	would	might		

Will and *would* are often contracted ('*ll* and '*d*), especially in speech. Each modal in the second row can serve as a past tense form for the one above, though that is not their only use. In addition, there are two verbs which operate like modals in some uses — namely, *need* and *dare*:

> That need not necessarily be so.

> I dare say that's true.

Most of the modals can be used to express degrees of certainty, as these examples illustrate:

That can happen at times.	It may rain this afternoon.
You could be right.	That might be the bus coming now.
That should be the one.	That'll be the bus now.
That ought to be enough.	John must have left.
Sally would be finished by now.	

However, modals can also be used to express a range of other meanings, including modulation (discussed later in this chapter). They can also be combined with other ways of expressing modality, as in this return to the unfortunate budgerigar:

The bird must certainly be dead.

This particular example appears to express a high degree of certainty, but even though the certainty is specially marked — perhaps because the fact had been questioned — the statement doesn't have the absolute certainty of *The bird is dead*.

It is also possible to modify a negative statement — for example:

The bird is probably not dead.

I doubt if the passionfruit would have fallen down behind the seat.

The passionfruit could hardly have fallen down behind the seat.

Modality is a way of marking the speaker's degree of certainty about the information. Yet it also comes to be used as a device marking the speaker's approach to the addressee, a ploy in the interaction. For instance, we might underplay our certainty about a piece of information because we are anxious not to alarm or offend our listeners.

Demanding goods and services

Interacting with other people and getting on in the world isn't just a matter of exchanging information. There's also the exchange of goods and services — getting things done and getting what you want. This may sound very aggressive and acquisitive, and that's one aspect we'll deal with in this section. However, it can all be done more subtly, including everything from persuasive coercion to friendly encouragement. That's an aspect we'll deal with in the next section.

In the exchange of goods and services, one very common way of using language is the command, which we touched on in Chapter 1. This category of meaning has its own characteristic structure known as the **imperative**. Here are some examples:

Stop.	Drive slowly.
Give it to me.	Call me Madam.
Rise and shine.	Be quiet.

Help me move this piano.   Return to sender.

Press in and pull back.   (instructions for opening a package)

These imperative clauses differ from the declarative structure used for making statements in a quite specific way, as we can see by comparing these examples:

They bring the paper every Saturday.   *(declarative)*

Bring the paper every Saturday.   *(imperative)*

In the imperative clause there is no subject in the position that *they* occupies in the declarative clause. In other words, the imperative leaves the subject unstated and begins with the verb group.

Yet the imperative clause does have a kind of hidden subject, the unstated *you* which is said to be 'understood'. This is because an imperative clause is normally used to convey a command, a directive or a piece of advice to someone who's expected to carry it out. So, *Bring the paper every Saturday* might be addressed as an instruction to a newsagent, who is the unstated *you*. As we noted in the last chapter, we can test for this unstated subject by adding a tag:

Bring the paper every Saturday, won't you?   Give it to me, will you?

However, it is possible to give instructions to people with the *you* included, as in:

You stop talking!   You give it to me!

These clauses are not imperative in structure. The only way we could be sure they were being used as commands would be from their context and from the tone in which they were said. The exclamation marks in the written versions are an attempt to convey that tone.

Sometimes we do specify the person to whom a command is addressed — in this way:

Hey you! Help me move this piano.

B Company! Present arms!

Ken, finish washing the car, will you?

Passengers wishing to alight, please be ready to do so.

In these examples, the opening which identifies the addressees may be called a **vocative** — a device for nominating or appealing to someone. But, as the punctuation suggests, it is not part of the imperative clause itself. The imperative structure still begins with the verb group and has no stated subject.

There are occasions when we rearrange the order of components in an imperative clause to bring something into greater prominence. However, although this means that the verb group doesn't come at the beginning, the clause still doesn't have an explicit subject. For example:

Every Saturday, bring the paper.

Carefully cut the fruit into small pieces.

Before we leave the imperative structure, we should stress a few general points. Exchanging goods and services plays an important part in human interaction and we use language in many ways in this exchange. The imperative structure plays a key role: it is used in giving commands and directives, making requests, offering advice and warnings, and setting out instructions and procedures. At the same time we must recognise that several other structures can be used for the same purposes, as the next section will show.

Modulation: the grammar of the velvet glove

Besides the factual *yes* and *no* of the exchange of information ('Yes, it is', 'No, it isn't'), there is the directive *yes* and *no* of the exchange of goods and services ('Yes, you can', 'No, you can't'). And just as informational clauses can be modified in the ways that we've already discussed, so the commands and offers of the exchange of goods and services can be modified in many ways to impose obligations, make requests and suggestions, and declare intentions. Between the directive *yes* and the directive *no* there lies a whole range of possible meanings (referred to generally as *modulation*), which can be expressed through a rich variety of grammatical resources. They play a big part in the interaction that goes on between people in many situations.

As an example, take a straight-out command, in both its positive and negative versions:

Get a new job.   Don't get a new job.

These are both quite clear and peremptory and both use the imperative structure. Their messages are not modulated in any way — not in their wording at any rate, though they could be spoken in various ways to allow intonation to modify their effect. But in interaction with other people we often do modify the directness of such messages by using the range of grammatical resources available to us — that is, by changing the wording. Here are some examples of modulation, ranging in function from imposing an obligation to making a suggestion:

You must get a new job.

You have to get a new job.

You ought to get a new job.

It's necessary for you to get a new job.

You should get a new job.

You are advised to get a new job.

You might get a new job.

You could get a new job.

Why don't you get a new job?

What about getting a new job?

Suppose you get a new job.

There's a difference between imposing an obligation on someone — something they may not want to do — and granting them permission to do something that they do want to do. But modulation is involved in each case:

You ought to go home now.   (to a guest who has overstayed his welcome)

You may go home now.   (to a group of school students)
You can go home now.
You are allowed to go home now.

Another kind of modulated command is the request, which can vary greatly in the degree of politeness and formality. Compare:

Close the door.

with:

Close the door, please.

Please close the door.

Would you please close the door?

Would you mind closing the door?

Would you be kind enough to close the door?

Although the last three involve the interrogative structure, they function as requests rather than questions. Whether or not they are written with question marks depends on the force of the request.

All of the examples considered so far can be seen as variations on a basic imperative structure where *you* (the addressee) is the unstated subject: in the modulated versions the subject becomes stated. Clauses with other subjects (e.g. *I*, *we* or a third-person subject) can also be modulated to express varying degrees of intention or obligation — for example:

I will get a new job.

I must get a new job.

I might get a new job.

The grammar of modulation

If we look at the structures used in all these examples, we can see that there are several types. Some make use of modal auxiliaries:

You should get a new job.

Others make use of a more complex structure which puts the basic process (*getting a new job*) into a subsidiary position in the clause, following *to* or *that*:

You are obliged to get a new job.

It's necessary for you to get a new job.

It's vital that you get a new job.

Then there are other possibilities, such as using the imperative *suppose* or an interrogative structure:

> Suppose you get a new job.
>
> Why don't you get a new job?

In fact the grammatical resources for expressing modulation are similar to those available for modality. We won't examine every detail of these structures, but some of the modal auxiliaries do need further comment here.

Modal ambiguity

Several of the modals can be used in more than one sense. Often the one modal can serve both the exchange of information, where it affects the modality of the clause, and the exchange of goods and services, where it affects the modulation. Here are straightforward examples of each, using *should*:

> Police said that the efforts of volunteer bushfire fighters in the past few days should be helped by a cool change in the weather today. *(modality)*

> Police said that the efforts of volunteer bushfire fighters in the past few days should be publicly commended. *(modulation)*

However, the use of *should* for both modality and modulation can lead to ambiguity; take this clause, for example:

> Dinner should be ready by now.

Two meanings are equally possible:

> 1) It is likely that dinner is now ready. *(modality)*
>
> 2) It is time for dinner to be ready. *(modulation)*

Must has the same potential for ambiguity:

> You must be very careful.
>
> 1) There is no doubt that you are very careful.
>
> 2) It is necessary for you to be very careful.

The second meaning (imposing an obligation) can also be expressed as:

> You have to be very careful.

But these days there's a tendency, especially in colloquial contexts, to use *have to* for modality to achieve special emphasis — for example:

> She has to be one of the best swimmers in the world.

This is often further modified, as in:

> She would have to be one of the best . . .

With your permission . . .

One of the greatest misconceptions about the uses of the modals in English is the belief that *can* is only to be used with reference to ability and should not be used for permission. This misconception has been perpetuated by generations of teachers and school textbooks, even though it is contrary to common usage. Consider these examples:

> Can I borrow your lawn-mower?
>
> Can I walk on it yet?
>
> Can you swim the length of the pool?

The first is a question of permission, not ability. Indeed, we don't normally ask questions about our own ability, except perhaps in situations where it depends on someone else's judgement. For instance, if you had injured your leg, you might at some stage say to the doctor (as in the second example), *Can I walk on it yet?* Yet even here it seems that what's involved is a combination of ability and permission. On the other hand, we do ask about other people's ability, as in the third example.

We can sum this up by saying that *can* is used both in the exchange of information, where it affects modality (e.g. ability, possibility), and in the exchange of goods and services, where it affects modulation (e.g. permission). Likewise *may* can be used for both kinds of meaning, as these examples show:

> It may rain tomorrow.   *(modality — possibility)*
>
> May I borrow your lawn-mower?   *(modulation — permission)*

Yet though the use of *may* in seeking permission closely resembles the use of *can*, it usually sounds more polite. Politeness is another aspect of interpersonal meaning — it expresses a more considerate attitude on the part of the speaker.

Just as there have been attempts to prescribe the use of *can* and *may*, there have been attempts to explain the difference between *shall* and *will* in simple terms. However, *shall* is not very common in Australian English, although it can be used — often to express strong intention or determination. *Will* is more common as a marker of intention, prediction or simple futurity and it is very often contracted to *'ll*, except where it is stressed.

A note on links with traditional grammar

Much of this chapter has been devoted to the ways in which both informative and directive clauses can be modified through modality and modulation respectively. These are uses of language which are not clearly identified in traditional grammar.

We have also considered the imperative structure, which is well accepted in traditional grammar. However, in the approach adopted in this book it is set in the context of the exchange of goods and services, where it can be seen as one of several structures used for expressing not only commands but also requests, warnings, advice and instructions.

CHAPTER 5

Processes, Transitivity and Participant Roles

We now return to the major function of language that was opened up in Chapter 2: the *experiential* function, or language as a reflection of the world. Through this function we are able to refer to the various aspects of our experience, including not only 'things' (i.e. actual things, people, concepts, etc.) but also processes and circumstances — all the elements of our experience that can be represented by the components of clauses. In Chapter 2 we began to see what resources our language offers us for this purpose, and we must now consider each type of component in more detail. We'll start by looking at the process component, the verb group, since this is the one that's the essential basis for the clause. However, first we'll introduce two further example texts.

TEXT 5.1 AN EXTRACT FROM A NEWSPAPER ARTICLE ON DRUGS

I was walking along Sutter Street in San Francisco, in broad daylight, close to the usually safe Japantown. A gang of black youths were walking in the opposite direction. They were well-fed and dressed in smart track suits and casual clothes — not your usual derelict types who would push the streetwise button of a visitor.

I made eye contact with one of them, as he was trying to attract my attention by wild gesticulation. What happened next was a blur of movement and pain. I was kicked in the stomach and punched in the eye. As I fell to the ground, I saw the youths run.

They were not interested in my money. They were not muggers. They were high, possibly on crack. They were engaging in a self-designed, juvenile 'hit-a-white-and-get-away-with-it' initiation ritual. I just happened to be the bloke with the whitest skin on the block.

TEXT 5.2 AN EXTRACT FROM A MAGAZINE ARTICLE ON MACADAMIA NUTS

The two [macadamia] species which produce edible nuts have quite distinctive characteristics. *M. integrifolia*: this is the smooth-leaf species, having a smooth or wavy margin to the leaves. The leaves are in whorls of three at each node and each leaf has a stem. Blossoms are creamy white. The nuts have a smooth glossy surface and are spherical. *M. tetraphylla*: the name means four leaves, referring to the grouping of the leaves in fours at each node. The leaves are sessile — without stems — being attached directly to the branches. The leaves have spiny or prickly margins and are sometimes quite long, up to 50 cm. Blossoms are pink to red when fully opened. The nuts have a more or less rough, pebbled surface and may be pointed at one end.

Types of process

In every clause there is a process, expressed by the verb group, on which the message of the clause hinges. There are several different types of process, distinguished by the different kinds of meaning they represent.

Material processes

Processes which express some action going on, some event or something happening are known as **material processes**. They are closest to the traditional description of the verb as 'a doing word'. This kind of process is a dominant feature of Text 5.1, from which two of these examples are drawn:

> I was walking along Sutter Street.
>
> I was kicked in the stomach.
>
> Our cat killed the neighbour's budgerigar.
>
> The lights were switched off at midnight.

Very similar to these material processes are the **behavioural processes**, concerned with aspects of behaviour which are in effect physiological processes (and so not necessarily subject to deliberate control):

> I can hardly breathe.
>
> She laughed, she cried, she damn near died.

Mental processes

Processes which involve thinking, feeling and perceiving are known as **mental processes**. The examples below illustrate the three sub-types:

processes of thinking (cognitive)

> He believed in God.
>
> Do you know the road rules?
>
> I can't understand this book.

processes of feeling (affective)

> I like Aeroplane Jelly.

> She loves me; she loves me not.
>
> They wanted to go overseas.

processes of perceiving

> We could hear the noise of the traffic on the highway.
>
> Can you feel any pain?
>
> I saw the youths run.

Some mental processes lead to the words of a message presented as part of a person's thoughts or state of mind, as in these examples:

> She thought she would be home for dinner.
>
> She hoped she would be home for dinner.
>
> He believed he had a good case.
>
> They thought they'd seen him on the premises.
>
> I don't understand what's happening.

Verbal processes

The presentation of the words of such messages can equally well follow a **verbal process** — that is, one associated with saying or some similar use of language:

> She said: 'I'll be home for dinner.'
>
> She said she'd be home for dinner.
>
> The prosecution alleged that he had been seen on the premises.
>
> The defendant said nothing.
>
> They were asked to leave.
>
> 'What's happening?' I asked.
>
> My watch says it's half past three already.

As these examples suggest, the 'speaker' is normally a person, although the last example shows that's not always the case. What issues from the verbal process may be either some abstract 'thing' — a way of using language like a *question* or an *answer*, or indeed *nothing* — or it may be the actual words said, like *'I'll be home for dinner'*, or else words which indirectly indicate what was said, such as *he had been seen on the premises*.

Relational processes

A small but very common group of processes establishes certain kinds of relationship. Text 5.2 includes many examples of these **relational processes**. One relationship they commonly establish is **attribution**. We can say that something has some quality; that is, we attribute the quality to the thing. In the examples that follow the attributes are indicated by **adjectives** (i.e. *creamy white, high, comfortable, comfy*), a class of words which will be discussed in the next chapter:

> Blossoms are creamy white.
>
> They were high, possibly on crack.
>
> This chair is very comfortable.
>
> She looked very comfy.

A similar relationship is the **possessive**:

> Each leaf has a stem.
>
> The nuts have a smooth glossy surface.
>
> The car's got four new tyres.
>
> I've got the money.
>
> That book belongs to me.

The most basic of the relationships that can be expressed by a relational process is **identity**. Two things are presented as being identical, or one is presented as an instance of the other (as in a classification statement):

> This is the smooth-leaf species.
>
> The name means four leaves.
>
> They were not muggers.
>
> He seems quite a nice chap.
>
> The ideal position for reading is something you can never find.

Some relational processes can also be used in clauses which assert the existence of something (they commonly begin with *there*). This is a rather different use of these processes because there is effectively only one participant. It is referred to as the **existential** use of the verbs concerned.

> There's a lighthouse on the headland.
>
> There seems to be some mistake.
>
> Once upon a time there were three bears.

In summary, we can say that there are several types of process, which are set out below:

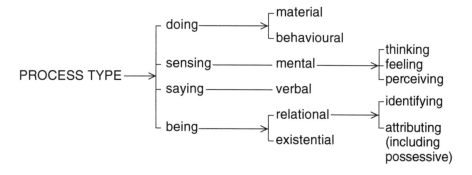

A system network of process types

Transitivity

As we saw in Chapter 2, the clause represents certain aspects of experience which are related through the process — a grammatical relationship referred to as the *transitivity* of the clause. Each of type of process can indicate a relationship between two or more things, ideas, messages and so on. However, apart from the purely relational processes, the *notion* of relationship is not generally predominant. Rather, the specific type of relationship is indicated by the process itself — that is, by the meaning of the verb — as usually the particular process is an important part of our experience. We can even have processes where the idea of relationship between two things (participants) is not involved at all:

> I'm thinking.
>
> It's raining.
>
> The dinner's cooking.
>
> The colour's changing.

In these, the process (the meaning of the verb) is predominant and the idea of relationship between two things is not relevant. At the other extreme are the relational processes which do little more than establish a relationship.

So there are two aspects to the meaning of the process: the process aspect and the relationship. Because 'relationship' is a rather general term which can apply to many aspects of grammar, we have a specific term for this kind of relationship within the clause — that is, *transitivity*. Transitivity is a most important aspect of the representation of our experience in language, for it is the means whereby we can bring things together to form messages.

Processes and the roles of participants

The essential point about transitivity is that things can be related together by being involved in a process. They 'participate' in the process and so are known as *participants*. As explained in Chapter 2, the term *participant* is being used here in a wider sense than it is generally: it includes not just people but anything that can get involved in a process. Here are some examples, with the participants in italics:

> *They* were not interested in *my money.*
>
> *Honesty* is *the best policy.*
>
> *The soldier* said: *'What will you tell your wife?'*
>
> *Their house* was burnt down.
>
> There were *no suspicious circumstances.*
>
> *The two species* have *quite distinct characteristics.*
>
> *What happened next* was *a blur of movement and pain.*

The different ways in which participants may be involved in a process can be described in terms of a small number of key roles, which we'll now consider.

Agent

Most processes are initiated or put into operation by some 'thing' (often a person) and this participant is described as the **agent**. For example, *our cat* is the agent in both these clauses:

> *Our cat* killed the neighbour's budgerigar.

> The neighbour's budgerigar was killed by *our cat*.

The agent isn't necessarily placed first in the clause, though it very often is. But no matter where it's placed, it will still have the same meaning relationship to the other components of the clause (i.e. it will initiate the process) despite changes in grammatical forms.

In some messages, however, the agent isn't mentioned at all, even though we know that the process must have been initiated somehow:

> Our neighbour's budgerigar got killed.

> The car was stolen.   (*cf. Someone* stole the car.)

Effect

A second way in which a participant can be involved in a process is as the result or outcome. There are several ways in which a participant can take on this role, and they depend largely on the type and meaning of the process. Compare these three examples:

> The chef made *the cake*.

> We all admired *the cake*.

> The children ate *the cake*.

A participant can be the effect of the process (i.e. effected by it), as in *The chef made the cake*, or it can be something affected by the process, as in *We all admired the cake*. Nevertheless, whichever it is for any specific process, we refer to its role as the **effect**. Here are some more examples:

> Mrs Cagney sold *her chairs*.

> *The neighbour's budgerigar* was killed by you know who.

> *I* was kicked in the stomach.

> The two species produce *edible nuts*.

> *The pies* were selling well.

> Let's get *some peanut brittle*.

> She said: *'Let's get some peanut brittle.'*

As with the agent, so with the effect — it's not the position in the clause which determines a participant's role but its relationship to the process.

Beneficiary

We'll approach the third role by way of two more examples, the first of which has three participants:

> Someone gave Charlie an old piano.

An old piano was given to Charlie.

An old piano is the effect in each clause and *someone* is the agent in the first (it's suppressed in the second). So where does that leave Charlie? He's not the agent and he's not the effect but he did get the piano. He represents the third role that participants can have in relation to the process — namely, the **beneficiary**.

So far we have identified three roles for participants:

  agent (AG)   *effect* (EF)   *beneficiary* (BN)

All three roles can be found in the one clause, and they remain constant whatever their position in the clause:

The lady	left	the rowing boat	to the young man.
AG		EF	BN

The rowing boat	was left	to the young man	by the lady.
EF		BN	AG

The young man	was left	the rowing boat	by the lady.
BN		EF	AG

The lady	left	the young man	the rowing boat.
AG		BN	EF

Entity

The three roles already introduced, especially agent and effect, are associated with material, verbal and mental processes. There is one other participant role, associated specifically with relational processes, which is referred to as the **entity**. Consider these examples:

Her husband was very tall.

Blossoms are pink to red.

The italicised 'thing' in each of these sentences doesn't appear to be playing any of the roles we have just discussed. It's not obviously initiating a process (the role of agent), nor can it be described as the effect — and it's certainly not a beneficiary. In fact, both *her husband* and *blossoms* are simply entities in a relationship; specifically they are being related to an attribute (i.e. *very tall* and *pink to red*). However, other relationships are possible, as these sentences show:

My old man's a dustman.

This is *the smooth-leaf species.*

The leaves have *spiny or prickly margins.*

In these examples a relationship is being established between two entities. However, in an existential clause there is only one entity, as in this example:

There was *a police car* following us.

This clause can be compared with the more straightforward *A police car was following us,* in which *a police car* is the agent and *us* is the effect. By contrast, in the existential clause introduced by the dummy subject *there* (not a participant), *a police car* is the single entity; *following us* is a non-finite clause (to be discussed in Chapter 9).

The next example with a relational process has two entities:

> You are *what you eat.*

Here one of the entities (*what you eat*) is a clause in its own right, but it is a clause functioning as a participant within another clause. As a clause it has its own participants with their own roles: *you* is the agent and *what* is the effect. As a participant in the larger clause it has a subsidiary role: *what you eat* is one entity.

Now consider this sentence:

> *The two species which produce edible nuts have quite distinctive characteristics.*

Here the first entity is a noun group containing the clause *which produce edible nuts.* That clause has its own agent *which,* its process *produce* and its effect *edible nuts.* The word *which* (the agent) refers to *the two species* and takes its meaning from this smaller noun group on which the larger group is based. Again, then, the clause *which produce edible nuts* is not a participant in itself, but only part of a participant.

In summary, the four participant roles are:

agent the participant which initiates the process

effect the result or outcome of the process, or what is affected by it

beneficiary the participant which benefits from the process

entity the participant involved in a relational or existential process.

This description of participant roles is based on Halliday (1985, pp. 101–37). However, it is a considerable simplification of his account and it blurs some distinctions. In particular, it blurs his point that participant roles are directly related to process types. It is thus a more rudimentary account of the functions of participants than Halliday's.

Participant roles and grammatical case

Readers familiar with traditional grammar may be thinking that these participant roles are like the traditional categories of *subject* and *object.* However, there are significant differences, as we can begin to see if we compare these examples:

1) The policeman found the lost girl.
2) The lost girl was found by the policeman.
3) He found her.
4) She was found by him.

In the first two clauses *the policeman* is the agent and *the lost girl* is the effect. The same applies in clauses 3 and 4 (assuming that the pronouns refer to the policeman and the lost girl). The roles of agent and effect are aspects of the meaning of the clauses. However, in clauses 3 and 4 there is a formal distinction between *he* and *him* and between *she* and *her*. These participants fit into the grammatical structure of each clause in a different way and the difference is marked by the forms of the pronouns. This grammatical distinction applies to clauses 1 and 2 as well, though it's not evident in the form of the words.

In clause 1 *the policeman* is the subject of the clause as well as being the agent — that is, 'The policeman' is the answer to the question 'Who found the lost girl?' and it is the policeman who initiated the action. In clause 2 the event is presented from a different viewpoint. If we ask the question 'Who was found by the policeman?', the answer is 'The lost girl'. So *the lost girl* is the subject of this clause. But even though the viewpoint is changed in clause 2, the experiential meaning is the same: the lost girl is still the effect of the process and the policeman is still the agent. The same applies to clauses 3 and 4, where the subjects are *he* and *she* respectively, as is shown by the use of those forms of the pronouns rather than *him* and *her*.

In the changed viewpoint of clause 2 the action of finding is looked at from the receiving end. This involves a change of grammatical structure whereby *the lost girl* becomes the subject of the clause and the verb group is changed to the **passive**. The verb group in the original clause is said to be **active**.

In clause 1 *the lost girl* is the **object** of the verb — i.e. what the action leads to. In clause 2 the verb has no object, but the word *by* does have one: namely, *the policeman*. Again it is the change of viewpoint that leads to grammatical changes from one clause to the other. In clauses 3 and 4 the pronoun forms *her* and *him* show that they too are objects. These grammatical categories, *subject* and *object*, are referred to as **cases**; in traditional grammar the subject is said to be in the *nominative* case and the object in the *objective* (or *accusative*) case.

However, the experiential meaning does not change: the roles of *the policeman* and *the lost girl* remain the same, agent and effect respectively. The change is a grammatical one. Subject and object are essentially grammatical categories; they arise from grammatical relationships within the clause. Yet grammar is not independent of meaning, and the choice of active or passive in clauses such as these could be determined by the way they fit into the rest of the text. It could thus be part of the larger textual meaning.

The various relationships and categories can be summarised thus:

| 1) | The policeman | found | the lost girl. |
| 3) | He | found | her. |

subject	verb group (active)	object
agent	*material process*	*effect*

2) The lost girl	was found	by	the policeman.
4) She	was found	by	him.

subject	verb group (passive)	object of *by*
effect	*material process*	*agent*

In clauses 1 and 3, where the verb is active, the distinction between the two types of category (participant role and grammatical case) is not obvious. The agent is the subject and the effect is the object. But in clauses 2 and 4, where the verb is passive, the two types of category are clearly not parallel. The agent is not the subject, nor is the effect the object.

None of these categories (subject/object or agent/effect) makes any difference to the form of the noun in English. The nouns in clauses 1 and 2 have the form *policeman* and *girl* irrespective of their category in the clause. But many of the pronouns in English do mark the distinction between subject and object; they have different forms for each case. The following table shows how this works out:

subject	object
I	me
you	you
he	him
she	her
it	it
we	us
they	them
who	who *or* whom

Only *you* and *it* do not vary, while the pronoun *who* has an optional form *whom*, which is used in some more formal contexts.

There is one grammatical case which is formally marked in the noun. This is the possessive case, which will be dealt with in Chapter 7. Pronouns also mark the possessive case — in fact most pronouns have two forms of possessive. However, the possessive normally establishes a relationship within the noun group, not at the level of the clause, and so it's not likely to be confused with participant roles.

Voice, viewpoint and focus

The verb groups in the clauses discussed in the previous section were described as *active* (in clauses 1 and 3) and *passive* (in clauses 2 and 4). These terms refer to a feature of the verb group well recognised in traditional grammar: what is known as *active* and *passive voice*. Many verbs have these two sets of forms, which allow for a useful variation in the clause.

One function of the passive is to avoid mentioning the agent — perhaps because it is unknown or can be taken for granted, or perhaps because it is being concealed. Some examples of this have been cited earlier in this chapter:

> The car was stolen.
>
> Our neighbour's budgerigar got killed.
>
> An old piano was given to Charlie.

These can be referred to as **agentless passives**. However, the suppression of the agent is not the most important function of the passive. More significant is that it allows for a change of viewpoint or focus, as illustrated in the previous section. It means that either the agent or the effect can be the first participant in the clause. It also means that we can position something at the end of a clause for extra emphasis. This positioning within the clause is often influenced by the neighbouring clauses and sentences — in other words, by how the clause fits into the development of the whole text (an issue we'll take up in Chapter 11).

Forming the passive

The active forms of the verb are the unmarked forms (i.e. the 'ordinary' or basic forms) and so the passive has to be marked in some special way. There are two ways of forming a passive in English, the *be* passive and the *get* passive. Both require the use of a form of the main verb known as the **past participle**.

For all regular verbs in English the past participle is the same as the past tense form — that is, in the written mode *-ed* or *-d* is added to the basic form (see Chapter 8 for further details). However, as their name implies, irregular verbs behave differently, and many (including some very common verbs) have a special form for the past participle which is different from the past tense form. Below are some examples, showing both the past tense and the past participle forms. The first three verbs are regular; the others are irregular.

basic form	past tense	past participle
walk	walked	walked
smile	smiled	smiled
wait	waited	waited
leave	left	left
find	found	found
catch	caught	caught
know	knew	known
swim	swam	swum
take	took	taken

Most dictionaries give the past tense and past participle forms of irregular verbs, often in brackets after the basic form. With some verbs the conventions for these forms are changing and there is some regional and social variation (for details, see Quirk et al. 1985, pp. 103–20).

The be *passive*

An active form can be converted into a passive by using the past participle and adding a form of the auxiliary *be* (*am, is, are, was, were*, etc.):

> I was kicked in the stomach.
>
> The path was being hosed down.
>
> Have you ever been dumped by a wave?
>
> She is expected to accept the offer.
>
> The college will be built on the site of the old jail.

The get *passive*

An active form can also be made passive by using the past participle and adding a form of the verb *get* (*gets, got*, etc.):

> I got kicked in the stomach.
>
> They were getting splashed by passing cars.
>
> You will get pushed around.

The *get* passive is less common than the *be* passive and is more colloquial.

Middle voice

There is another way of changing the focus of a clause without using a formal passive. Compare:

> | Ambrose is cooking the dinner. | *(active)* |
> | The dinner is being cooked by Ambrose. | *(passive)* |
> | The dinner is being cooked. | *(agentless passive)* |
> | The dinner is cooking. | *(middle)* |

Both the last two examples describe something happening without mentioning any agent, but in the last an agent is not even implied (as it is in the agentless passive). In both *the dinner* remains the effect (as in the first two examples), but in the last the form of the verb group is active. This distinctive use, which throws the whole emphasis on the process, is quite common in some contexts and can be referred to as the **middle voice**. Here are some further examples:

> The kettle's boiling.   The pies are selling well.

The middle voice is also used in an abbreviated form in signs like NOW SHOWING (of a film) or NOW LEASING (of office accommodation).

Conclusion

In this chapter we have been concerned with processes and the participants associated with them. This has involved some aspects of the grammar of both verb groups and noun groups. These two important structures are further explored in the next three chapters — noun groups in Chapters 6 and 7, and verb groups in Chapter 8.

The Noun Group: Pinning Things Down

In the representation of our experience it is perhaps the 'things' which are most obvious — the things (including people, concepts, etc.) which can take on participant roles in messages about the world. In earlier chapters we have begun to consider the resources our language offers us in this area. We must now look at them more closely and explore their richness and adaptability.

How to talk about every thing in the world

As we use language to represent our experience, we constantly need to refer to 'things' in the world. English is well supplied with resources enabling us to do this, and the resources are of two kinds:

- lexical resources (i.e. words, parts of words, set phrases)
- grammatical resources (i.e. structures, word forms, structure words).

The term **lexical** refers to the *lexicon* or vocabulary of the language. We usually think of the vocabulary of a language as its stock of words. However, we should also include two other kinds of element: meaningful parts of words and those word groups and phrases which have become set expressions in the language.

The basic elements in the vocabulary are really the meaningful parts of words. These smallest meaningful elements in the language are known as **morphemes**. They include things like prefixes (e.g. *un-* in *unsafe*), suffixes (e.g. *-ly* in *safely*) and the bases to which they are attached (e.g. *safe*), as well as short words not divisible into smaller elements (e.g. *bread*). They also include the grammatical endings which produce the different forms of some words (e.g. *-ed* in *walked*). Thus morphemes are relevant to both the lexical and the grammatical resources of the language. The ways in which different word forms are made up is referred to as **morphology**.

For many of the things we need to talk about we have a single word which means that particular thing. The words with this kind of meaning are *nouns*. They constitute a very extensive class of words in the language — a class that is constantly being added to as new words come into use. In referring to the things in our world we can usually make some progress by using these nouns that exist ready-made for us. A children's riddle may underline the point:

> Q. What are watermelons called in Louisiana?
>
> A. Watermelons.

However, we very often find that nouns by themselves are inadequate, for we usually want to represent our experience in such detail that we have to go beyond the lexical resources of the language. And when there's no single word for things we want to talk about (or we don't know what it is), we turn to that other great resource, the grammatical structures. We construct a word group.

Take an example or two. We have a word *sandwich*, but we have no single word that means a *corned beef and pickle sandwich*. For that we use a word group which draws on our resources of vocabulary (including *corned*, *beef*, *pickle* and *sandwich*) and which is based on a structure that is part of the language's grammatical resources. The same principle applies to more elaborate or exotic examples like *an itsy-bitsy teeny-weeny yellow polka-dot bikini* (from an old song). Many of the word groups we use exist ready-made like the single words, but we also make up word groups as required. The part of the grammar describing these larger structures is sometimes referred to as **syntax** (in contrast to morphology, which is the grammar of word forms).

In some fields we have many single nouns with specific meanings which we can use if we are familiar with that field. We are then drawing on the lexical resources of the language — the vocabulary. But if we don't know these words or don't want to use them, we can still make up word groups for referring to the same kind of thing. We are then using the grammatical resources to construct a more specific reference. The particular structure available for this is the *noun group* (a term, you will remember, which can include nouns used by themselves). Overleaf are some examples referring to different kinds of horses. Most of the noun groups in the right-hand column draw on a simpler and more widely shared vocabulary, though this needn't necessarily be so.

lexical	grammatical (syntactic)
a stallion	a male horse
a mare	a female horse
a foal	a very young horse
a colt	a young male horse
a filly	a young female horse
a yearling	a one-year-old horse
a gelding	a castrated horse
a brumby	a wild horse

In talking about these kinds of horses, then, we have the choice of lexical or grammatical resources. But as we become increasingly specific, we soon exhaust the lexical resources and must rely on grammatical structures of increasing complexity to make specific references. We simply don't have enough words in the language to refer to every facet of everyone's individual experience of the world. But then we don't need to because we can so readily formulate word groups, using a relatively limited range of grammatical structures together with the vocabulary we have. Thus, still talking about horses, we can make much more specific references by means of noun groups like these:

a black and white horse	the horse we used to ride
a piebald horse	the horse in the float
a racehorse	a racehorse named 'Run Jim Run'
a quarter horse	Alexander the Great's horse
that horse over under the tree	the horse that Lady Godiva rode
that horse coming up on the inside	

Groups like *a racehorse* and *a quarter horse* lie near the boundary between single words and set word groups. People might differ as to which side of the fence they put them, but of course that only becomes obvious in the written forms.

The capacity we have for producing noun groups gives our language use enormous potential. It's true that English has a very rich vocabulary of words for referring to 'things' (i.e. nouns), so that vocabulary size is sometimes thought to be a measure of a person's language competence, yet the potential offered by the grammatical structures of the noun group is far greater. These expandable structures allow us to represent in words a vast range of experience. Consequently, competence in using the structures of the language is a far more powerful resource than an extensive vocabulary. What really counts is not how many words you know but what you can do with them.

The expandable noun group

The noun group structure allows us to talk about virtually any 'thing' in the world by building on the basic resources of the vocabulary. It's really a cluster of structures, incorporating a whole range of potential components and sub-structures. It is extremely versatile, somewhat complex and almost infinitely expandable.

Except where a pronoun is being used, a noun group is always based on one key noun, which can be referred to as the **head noun** of the group. Other nouns may be included, but there will always be one basic noun (or pronoun). The main features of the noun group can be summarised like this:

pre-modifier	head noun	post-modifier
	pronoun	

Some noun groups consist of just a single noun by itself — as when one functions as a group by being a participant in a clause or a component in a phrase. The italicised words in these sentences are examples:

Trees are worth preserving.

They were smoking *marijuana*.

Margaret is the one who arrived late.

However, it's much more usual for the head noun to have something else with it, something which can modify the reference of the noun and so make it more specific. This extra something can come before the head noun (where it functions as a **pre-modifier**), or after it (a **post-modifier**). Some noun groups have both pre- and post-modifiers. Here are some examples:

pre-modifier	head noun	post-modifier
those	trees	
those beautiful old elm	trees	
those beautiful old elm	trees	lining the drive
the	trees	which line the drive
deciduous	trees	
	trees	which lose their leaves

Nouns can be modified in several different ways: that is, several different kinds of meaning can come into both the pre-modifier and post-modifier components of the group. In general, such meanings make the reference of the basic noun more specific, because by adding meaning we can narrow down the reference and make it more precise. In the following sections we'll consider some of these kinds of meaning, beginning with those that normally appear in the pre-modifier.

The very thing

In making reference to 'things' we are able to distinguish between two possibilities:

definite: the thing we refer to is a particular one of its kind

indefinite: the reference is to any instance of the thing, not to a
                  particular instance.

The difference is illustrated in these two sentences:

> She turned up in the red sports car.
>
> She turned up in a red sports car.

In the first example, with *the*, we understand that some particular red sports car already known to speaker and listener is involved. In the second example, with *a*, the red sports car may have been completely unexpected.

The word *the* is the basic marker of definiteness, and *a* (or *an*) is a common marker of the indefinite. These words are sometimes called the **definite** and **indefinite articles** respectively. However, they are not the only ways of marking a reference as definite or indefinite.

Several other words and word groups contain the notion of 'definite' as part of their meaning. We can have:

> this red sports car   that red sports car
>
> my red sports car   my brother's red sports car

These groups are just as definite as *the red sports car*. At the same time, the words *this*, *that* and *my* contain other elements of meaning besides definiteness, while *my brother's* includes *my brother*, a noun group in its own right.

There are also other ways in which we can mark indefiniteness:

> any red sports car   some red sports car (or other)
>
> red sports cars   some red sports cars

When a thing is first referred to in a text, it may be indefinite. Yet once it is introduced, any further references to it are definite because it is the particular instance of the thing already referred to. So, in Text 5.1, we have the noun group *a gang of black youths* in which both *gang* and *youths* are indefinite, but further down the writer refers to *the youths* — definite.

There are some nouns which don't have to be marked as definite because they are definite by their very nature — the indefinite possibility hardly arises. They include:

| *names:* | Perth | William Pitt | Sally | Indonesia |
| *abstractions:* | literacy | lunacy | health | happiness |

However, almost every time we make reference to something in the world of our experience, we mark our reference as definite or indefinite. This is why we usually need more than just a single noun by itself. We need a noun group consisting of at least a **pointer** as well as the noun. A pointer (or **deictic**) is usually one of a small group of words including *the, a, some* and *that* — words which in effect point to the noun they are associated with, as in these examples:

the apple	this crocodile
a book	that alligator
some chocolates	these snakes
any biros	those spiders

But pointers are not just concerned with marking the definite/indefinite option. There are other aspects of meaning involved as well: for example, notions of proximity and relevance indicated by words like *this* and *that*, and notions of possession with pointers like *my* and *your*.

The numbers game

When we refer to the things in our experience, it's often necessary to indicate the number of items involved. Our language comes well equipped for us to do this.

To begin with, we can modify the noun itself without adding anything to the pre-modifier component of the group. The basic form of the noun is the **singular**, but most nouns have a special form, the **plural**, which is used for references to more than one instance of the thing they represent. Having two forms, a singular and a plural, is one of the main formal features of nouns, and one of the criteria for identifying them.

Most nouns form their plural in the following way:

in speech: by adding the sounds -/s/ or -/z/ or the syllable - /əz/ (depending on how the singular ends)

in writing: by adding -*s* or -*es* (depending on how the singular ends)

street	streets	-/s/
road	roads	-/z/
church	churches	- /əz/
lane	lanes	-/z/
place	places	- /əz/

There are some nouns which form their plurals in a different way, such as the small number of very common nouns which change their vowel (e.g. *man, men*), or the less common words that retain a foreign plural (e.g. *formula, formulae*). With some of the latter there's a bit of wavering between the original plural and the regular English plural (e.g. *syllabi* or *syllabuses*); both plurals can be heard. If you're uncertain, it's generally better to use the English plural (the one written -*s* or -*es*).

The singular/plural distinction is only a very rough indication of number. However, we can be more specific about the number of items being referred to if we bring something into the pre-modifier of the noun group. For a start, there are the numbers themselves:

twenty-six sheep	the same four people
four and twenty blackbirds	two dozen eggs
four hundred paces	twenty sick sheep

Even if there's only one item, that can be specifically marked by using the number *one* (or a similar device) in the noun group:

one teacher (*cf.* a teacher)	one only 51cm television set
the one day of the year	a single diamond

It's also possible to refer to a number of items without indicating the exact number — sometimes we don't know the exact number and sometimes it's not necessary to be precise:

a few cars	a lot of semi-trailers
some buses	a number of wheel-chairs
several trucks	umpteen scooters
many bicycles	hundreds of skate-boards
lots of motorbikes	thousands of people

There are also more colloquial terms like *heaps of, oodles of, scads of* and *zillions of.*

The word *both* refers to the two items making up an identifiable pair. Compare these examples:

He had both legs bandaged.

He had two legs bandaged.

He had a couple of legs bandaged.

Both the last two examples suggest that 'he' had more than two legs which might have been bandaged.

Another useful device is one which enables us to refer both to a group of items and to each single item in the group at the same time. It sounds complicated but it's really quite simple — and it is very common. It's a way of emphasising that there are no exceptions:

Put six oysters on each plate.

Every model is in working order.

Words like *each* and *every* are both singular and plural. They are singular in that the noun which follows them is singular (as is any following verb), yet they convey the notions of inclusiveness and plurality. *Everyone* and *everybody* have the same characteristics as *each* and *every* but their noun is built in. However, the plural component in their meaning can affect the choice of a pronoun to refer back to them, as in:

Has everyone got *their* books out?

The notion of inclusiveness contained in the meaning of *every* can also be expressed by the word *all*, which in these instances takes a plural noun:

> All the models are in working order.

However, *all* can also be used with a certain group of singular nouns to refer to **amount** (rather than number), as in:

> Pour all the milk into the mixture.

All can be used in these two ways (with plural and singular nouns) because there are two distinct groups of nouns, one of which doesn't have a plural at all. This distinction will be explained when we consider count nouns and mass nouns later in the chapter.

The epithet

A noun group can also include one or more **epithets**. This element indicates some quality of the thing being referred to and it is realised by means of an *adjective* or a group of words based on an adjective. Adjectives are an important class of words available for referring to the qualities and characteristics of things, and they can be used both as attributes in relational clauses and as epithets within the noun group. The two possibilities can be illustrated by adapting an example introduced in Chapter 5:

> This chair is comfortable.   this comfortable chair

The adjective can itself be modified by an **intensifier** (e.g. *very, extremely*) or another **adverb** (a class of word discussed in Chapter 8):

> This chair is very comfortable.   this very comfortable chair
>
> The president is invariably busy.   the invariably busy president

Further examples can be found in Texts 5.1 and 5.2:

> the usually safe Japantown
>
> quite distinctive characteristics
>
> a more or less rough, pebbled surface

The epithet does not necessarily represent an objective, *experiential* quality; it may simply indicate the speaker's or writer's attitude to the thing, in which case it is an *interpersonal* epithet. For example:

> a delightful cottage (*cf.* an old cottage)
>
> a fantastic concert (*cf.* an expensive concert)

Some swear words are used in this interpersonal way — for example:

> The bloody car broke down.

In many cases the context will determine whether an epithet is experiential or interpersonal, and even then the distinction may be blurred (e.g. *a small cottage*).

The classifier

The head noun is often preceded by another word which classifies the thing being referred to. This word, known as a **classifier**, may be an adjective or it may be another noun (which in traditional grammar is known as 'a noun used as an adjective').

The use of classifiers is extremely common and adds to the versatility of the noun group. To begin with a homely example — if we're thinking of pies, we can have hot pies, cold pies, big pies, small pies, fresh pies, stale pies and so on. These are all qualities that a pie can have and they are indicated by epithets. But there are many different kinds of pie and we can classify them according to what's in them. We do this using a noun as a classifier:

    meat pies   apple pies

    mulberry pies   custard pies

We can also have noun groups which combine an epithet with a classifier:

    hot meat pies   large apple pies

As we focus on some of the details of our experience, it's possible to devise almost endless combinations of classifiers:

    round table discussions   the family car

    gut bucket jazz   poll hereford conferences

Bureaucratic and technical fields are especially rich in these combinations:

    mature age allowance   mature age partner allowance

    income equalisation deposit scheme

    small computer system interface port

    barrel locking nut   barrel locking nut retainer plunger

Adjectives which serve as classifiers are generally a different group from those which serve as epithets; they cannot be graded in the way that epithet adjectives can. A traditional (but not infallible) test is to ask whether an adjective can be combined with *very* (epithets can). It would work with these examples:

    a domestic cat   a feral cat   *(classifiers)*

    a fat cat   a skinny cat   *(epithets)*

However, some adjectives can be used in either function — for example, *wild* in this set:

    wild animal   domestic animal   *(classifiers)*

    wild animal   docile animal   *(epithets)*

Now consider this set:

    a music teacher   a musical teacher

    the music shop   musical instruments

In these examples the noun *music* functions as a classifier, denoting a class of teacher or shop. But the adjective *musical* shows that it can perform both functions: in *musical instruments* it is a classifier, distinguishing them from other classes of instrument; in *a musical teacher* it is an epithet, for musicality is an attribute and many teachers may be musical even though they are not music teachers.

Summing up the pre-modifier

The pre-modifier position allows for several kinds of modification — that is, it allows for several different kinds of meaning to specify the reference of the noun. They can be summarised thus:

pointer	the trees	a dairy
	some opium	that boy
numerative	four wives	seven brothers
	many months	few words
epithet	dirty linen	angry penguins
classifier	chocolate sauce	apple pie
	project homes	aluminium foil

Quite often several of these components are used together in the one noun group. They are normally used in the order given above, and so the pre-modifier part of the noun group comes to have a very predictable structure, as the following table of examples shows. There can be variations from this conventional order, but when there are, the change conveys a special emphasis on something in the group.

pointer	*numerative*	*epithet*	*classifier*	*head noun*
	six	white		horses
the		little red	school	house
a			lemon-scented	gum
	two		imported artificial	legs
that		battered	second-hand cassette	radio
a		lovely	chocolate-coated	iceblock
	several	ancient	musical	instruments

Note that none of these components of the pre-modifier is essential; indeed, some noun groups have no pre-modifier at all. Note too that if the epithet component includes a colour adjective, that usually follows any other quality.

The post-modifier

The post-modifier part of the noun group also allows for several possible structures to modify the head noun or the first part of the group. Some of

these structures apply to a relatively small number of well-known instances
— for example:

numerative	George VI (*spoken as* George the Sixth)
epithet	Alfred the Great
classifier	director general
identifying name	my son David

The more widely used structures are as follows:

phrase	the house on the hill
	the car in the photo
	a gang of black youths
non-finite clause	dolphins swimming ahead of the ship
	a newspaper delivered to the house
	an old gramophone picked up in a junk shop
finite clause	the house that Jack built
	the table which was left to me by my aunt
	the insect pests that damage crops

(The differences between finite and non-finite clauses will be explained in
Chapter 9.)

It is worth noting that in using a phrase or a clause to modify a noun we
are using structures which themselves contain noun groups, and that these
noun groups can in turn be modified. This may lead to some quite long and
sometimes complex structures — for example:

the long trill at the end of the cadenza of the slow movement of the D minor
concerto of Brahms

By using these post-modified noun groups, as well as the resources of
the pre-modifier, we are able to refer to things in highly specific ways,
allowing us to identify them more precisely for our listeners or readers.
Here are some further examples, beginning with some from Texts 5.1 and
5.2; in each case the head noun is italicised:

a smooth or wavy *margin* to the leaves

the *bloke* with the whitest skin on the block

a self-designed, juvenile 'hit-a-white-and-get-away-with-it' initiation *ritual*

the *destruction* by fire of the first church in Australia

that old two-storey high Victorian terrace *house* which is being restored
down near the bridge

the British theatre *critic* who wrote 'O Calcutta'

We'll end this section with an example of a sentence which contains
several complex noun groups:

The publisher John Calder, who with his then partner Marion Boyars was to
be immortalised for lawyers in 'R v. Calder and Boyars', a notable battle in

the long, hard-fought, often serious, sometimes important, frequently farcical, and occasionally trivial, war between the freedom of the written word and our legal system, had been one of the organisers of the playwrights' conference in Edinburgh.

(John Mortimer, *Clinging to the Wreckage*)

The basic sentence is:

The publisher John Calder had been one of the organisers of the playwrights' conference in Edinburgh.

The first noun group *the publisher John Calder* is followed by a long clause (*who . . .*) in which there are several noun groups, including one running all the way from *a notable battle* to *our legal system*. You might like to amuse yourself on a wet afternoon by identifying all the smaller noun groups which are brought together in various ways in this sentence.

Count nouns and mass nouns

As we've seen, the plural forms of nouns allow us to refer to more than one item of the category that the noun represents. However, there are some things that can't be counted off as discrete items because we think of them as an undifferentiated mass. They include such things as:

food	wheat	iron	traffic	bread	water

as well as abstractions like:

happiness	industrialisation	transubstantiation

Because of the kind of things that these nouns represent, they are called **mass nouns** or **non-countables,** in contrast to the nouns that refer to things occurring as discrete items, which are known as **count nouns** or **countables.**

This distinction between count nouns and mass nouns is different from the traditional distinction between 'common nouns' and 'collective nouns'. Since collective nouns (such as *group, team* or *council*) can have plural forms (*groups, teams, councils*), they are count nouns.

Mass nouns have no plural forms. And even with the singular forms we don't refer to single items of the categories they represent. We don't say *a food, one food* or *a single food* — we simply talk about *food*. But we do say things like:

all this food	enough food	too much food

This is because the mass noun can be included in a noun group indicating the quantity of materials involved. One way of doing this is to give a non-specific indication of quantity:

a little cheese	a lot of lettuce
too much milk	lots of jam
how much sugar?	plenty of soap

However, there is another way of indicating quantity that allows us to be quite specific: it can be expressed as a number of conventional units of measurement. The units themselves are countable and each unit represents an agreed amount of the material:

30 bushels of wheat	a thousand barrels of oil
3 kg of sugar	4 tonnes of flour

Here the mass noun is part of an *of* phrase, as it is in some of the non-specific examples in the previous group.

Before we leave this section, we should note that some mass nouns have an equivalent count noun, identical in its basic form, which can be used with *a* in the singular and also form a plural. This is especially the case with nouns referring to food and drink where several varieties are implied:

The Whiskies of Scotland	(book title)
JAMS AND SPREADS	(supermarket sign)

or where a conventional serve or measure is implied:

a beer	(e.g. a can of beer)
three coffees	(i.e. three cups of coffee)

How to avoid nouns

So far we have been looking at the way noun groups allow us to identify and refer to the things in our world of experience. We can also do this by means of the *reference pronouns*. You'll remember that the main ones are *he*, *she*, *it* and *they*, and their related forms. These are very commonly used for referring to things (including people), but they have to be used in conditions where the context makes it clear what or who they are referring to.

For convenience, the basic and related forms of the reference pronouns are set out below.

Basic forms	Related forms		
	objective	possessives	reflexive
he	him	his his	himself
she	her	her hers	herself
it	it	its its	itself
they	them	their theirs	themselves
one	one	one's –	oneself

The reference pronouns themselves give some hint of the kind of 'thing' they refer to, but they are not very specific and their basic meaning can be simply stated:

he	a male (including things figuratively presented as male)

she   a female (including things figuratively presented as female)

it   an inanimate object or an abstraction

they   all plural references, whether to men, women, other living things, objects or abstractions

one   the generalised person

The available choices of meaning can also be represented in the form of a network:

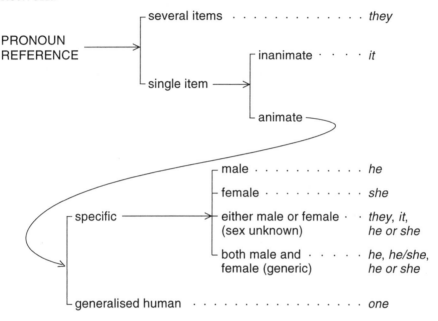

On examination this network reveals that the English language has a gender problem. There are some unfortunate gaps in the pronoun system. Meanings that we sometimes want to express don't have a single pronoun of their own and so we have to use pronouns that have more than one meaning. The resulting ambiguity can give people the wrong impression. It also accounts for the complexity down at the end of the single-animate-specific path in the network, which arises because of two similar problems:

1   It is difficult to refer to a single person when their sex is not known. I have to resort to *their* even to discuss the problem (*his or her* would look clumsy), and yet *their* is a pronoun we normally think of as plural. Admittedly a baby whose sex is unknown to the speaker is sometimes referred to as *it* (though preferably not in the hearing of the parents). But when we want to refer to *someone* or *everyone* with a reference pronoun, we generally use the normal plural form — certainly in speech and less formal writing:

Someone's left their jacket here. No doubt they'll come back for it.

Has everyone got their books out?

So *they* and its related forms, though normally having a plural reference, come to have a singular one as well because they are free of any gender reference. It's true that the use of *their* in *Has everyone got their books out?* can be explained in terms of the plural component in the meaning of *every*. However, this explanation does not apply to *someone*.

2   A much more contentious problem is that in English we have no suitable pronoun for singular human generic references. A generic reference is one which refers to every member of a category; it can be plural without a pointer (as in the first two examples below), or singular with *the* (as in the next two):

   Doctors used to be respected members of the community.

   Cars are unsafe at any speed.

   The doctor used to be a respected member of the community.

   The car is unsafe at any speed.

If we have to use a pronoun to refer back to one of these generic nouns, we have no difficulty with the plural generic because our plural pronoun *they* makes no distinction between the sexes. And with the inanimate singular (*the car*) human gender is irrelevant. But *the doctor* is another matter. Traditionally, for these singular human generics, the pronoun *he* has been used (and still is widely used):

   The doctor should have the respect of his patients.

But because *he* is also the pronoun used for referring to males, it may seem to exclude females even when being used generically. The plausible and offensive implication of the example above is that it excludes all women doctors.

   Some people resolve this problem by pluralising the generic and using *they*, which at least avoids the sex distinction. And since we can have plural generics anyway, this solution often seems appropriate. But it doesn't work in every instance; sometimes we want to emphasise the singular nature of the generic.

   The problems encountered with both *he* and *they* in the generic role have led to the more widespread use of *he or she* (sometimes written as *he/she* or even *s/he*). However, this is a slightly cumbersome way of getting round the difficulty — and the cumbersomeness becomes more obvious when there are several *he or she*s or *himself or herself*s in a row.

   All this highlights a deficiency in the English pronoun system. Or rather, it shows how our language reflects our social attitudes — in this case, changing social attitudes. There are certain meanings for which there is no one pronoun that does not also have some other meaning. There is no plural pronoun which refers to a single sex — nor even one which distinguishes people from inanimate objects. But more serious is the fact that we cannot refer to a single human being without getting involved in sex. And who knows where that will lead?

Getting Things Together

Besides using language to refer to the things in our experience, we use it to show how things are related to each other, making connections which enable us to build up a more or less coherent picture of the world. Some of the connections we make are established at the clause level through the relationship of transitivity, discussed in Chapter 5. Others can be established within the noun group, which we began to explore in Chapter 6. In this chapter we'll consider further relationships which can be indicated explicitly in the wording of the noun group. Some of them are very common features of English.

Addition and other alternatives

One group of relationships which can be established both within and between noun groups is known generally as **co-ordination**. These are the relationships marked by such words as *and*, *or* and *but*, and they are very common. The simplest of them is **addition**, the relationship between any two or more items which in some way go together. It is most simply expressed by means of *and*, as in:

> war and peace
>
> the shop at the corner and the place next door

Dual noun groups like these can be participants in a clause or they can fulfil any other noun group role — for instance, in a larger noun group or a phrase:

> Jack and Jill went up the hill.
>
> It was achieved by a process of trial and error.

> part of their Science and Social Studies units of work on
> Endangered Species and Hot-Wet Lands

It's also possible to have more than two noun groups brought together in this way, so that the items form a kind of list:

> doctors, lawyers, engineers and architects
>
> a low sofa, a few poufs and a drinks trolley

And is needed only between the last two items of such lists; in writing the others are separated by commas, while in speech the list can be marked by intonation — rising on each item except the last, which has a falling tone. But occasionally one encounters quite a complex list where not even the punctuation is enough to make the relationships clear on first reading:

> Buildings in prefabricated form, scientific equipment, tents, food, cloth-
> ing and aviation, heating and cooking fuel are just some of the materials
> and items which must be carried overland to sustain these camps.

Here a comma after *clothing* would help prepare the reader for the fact that *aviation, heating and cooking* are a subsidiary list of classifiers within a noun group which can be seen as one item in the main list.

The same noun group (*aviation, heating and cooking fuel*) illustrates the point that *and* can also be used to link components within the one noun group, either in the pre-modifier or the post-modifier. Here are some further examples:

> a bold and imaginative plan
>
> a remedy tried and true
>
> conduct prejudicial to good order and military discipline

And can also be used to link other components in the clause, such as circumstances, or two closely associated verb groups:

> The water was everywhere, in the garage and all through the house.
>
> People were yelling and shouting in the street outside.

Relationships of co-ordination between clauses (including the role of *and*) will be dealt with in Chapter 9.

Another relationship signalled by *and* can be seen by comparing these two examples:

> I like crumpets and muffins.   I like crumpets and honey.

The second is not a relationship of addition but one of **accompaniment** (a *with* relationship). In such statements the word *with* can often be substituted for *and* without substantially changing the meaning. Another way of distinguishing between addition and accompaniment is to expand the first example like this:

> I like crumpets and I like muffins.   I like both crumpets and muffins.

I like crumpets and honey cannot be paraphrased like this — or rather, if it were, it would seem unusual, not to say perverse. The reason is that the phrase *crumpets and honey* is typical of a very common type of ready-made collocation for things that are regularly associated:

bread and butter	fish and chips	cheese and biscuits
trial and error	rock 'n' roll	gin and tonic

In speech the *and* in these phrases is hardly more than the /n/ sound, sometimes written as *'n* or *'n'*. What they refer to is treated as one entity. Somewhat similar to these expressions is the linking of two colour adjectives within a noun group, as in:

a blue and white flag

Since it could not be both blue and white all over, we understand that this flag is partly blue and partly white.

Both/and *and* either/or

Besides the *and* relationships which we've been exploring, relationships of coordination include the *or* relationship, known as the **alternative** relationship. We can compare them with the help of a sign in a library:

Bent and illegible loan cards not accepted.

This could mean either:

loan cards which are *both* bent *and* illegible
     or
loan cards which are *either* bent *or* illegible

In other words, if we consider a single card, we have these possibilities:

a bent card	an illegible card	a bent and illegible card

Essentially the *and* relationship joins items together, while the *or* relationship presents a choice between them. However, it's quite common for the items in an *or* relationship to be virtually interchangeable, in which case the notion of choice may take second place to the notion of joining, shifting the meaning closer to that of the *and* structure.

The words *both* and *either* are optional elements in the structures; they serve to introduce and emphasise the relationships:

both cool and temperate climates   either sandy or muddy surfaces

Note, however, that *both . . . and* can only be used to join a pair of items, not items in a more extended list.

The examples above illustrate these relationships amongst epithets within a noun group. Yet they can also be applied to noun groups themselves, as well as to other components of the clause:

Rubbish will be collected both on Mondays and on Thursdays.

You can either have dessert or cheese and biscuits.

Sometimes more than two things are presented as alternatives; for this we have a list with *or* placed between the last two items:

> Would you like tea, coffee, a soft drink or something stronger?

Or lists can be considerably extended, especially if the notion of choice is secondary; this local council notice involves a whole string of noun groups:

> Household garbage, stoves, refrigerators, industrial and trade wastes, trade refuse, motor tyres, trees and tree branches, large stones, large pieces of concrete or bricks (builders' refuse) or any rubbish or material which is offensive, dangerous or too large to handle will not be removed.

Now let's consider an example with the negative of *either . . . or*. Unlikely though it may sound, this one really was addressed to a driver manoeuvring at a service station:

> Go through there, crashing into neither the Mazda nor the Porsche.

Another possibility is the exclusion of one item in favour of another. This is marked by *not . . . but*:

> Rubbish should be placed not in bags but in bins.

Indeed, it's possible for more than one item to be excluded, though not always with the rhetorical flourish of this example:

> their manner of writing is very peculiar, being neither from the left to the right like the Europeans; nor from the right to the left like the Arabians; nor from up to down like the Chinese; nor from down to up like the Cascagians, but aslant, from one corner of the paper to the other, like ladies in England.
>
> (Jonathan Swift, *Gulliver's Travels*)

We'll end this section by noting that there are several other words and phrases which can be used to indicate that something is being added or considered in addition to something else. These emphasise, elaborate or modify the meaning of *and*. They are italicised in the examples below:

> **in addition to and**
>
> All this and heaven *too* . . .
>
> Pick up the fruit — and *also* some milk.
>
> We'll take you and Jane *as well*.
>
> And *in addition* we can supply . . .

> **instead of and**
>
> You *along with* the rest should . . .
>
> Considering other drugs *as well as* marijuana . . .
>
> Persistence *together with* a little cunning . . .
>
> The heat *in addition to* their fatigue . . .
>
> . . . *plus* I want some rice.

Comparison

One of the ways in which we build up our picture of the world is to compare things. We set up relationships between things by presenting them as being the same, similar or different — either in a general way or on some specific basis.

Comparisons involving sameness, similarity or difference in a general way can be made with explicit phrases, such as these:

Your fridge is	the same as	ours.
	identical to	
	similar to	
	like	
	not the same as	
	different from	

Note, however, that there are two alternatives to the last phrase, *different from*: namely, *different to* and *different than*. All three are widely used. *Different than* is conventional in American English, while *different from* is traditionally preferred in Australian and British English on the grounds that it is also possible to say, *Your fridge differs from ours*, but not . . . *differs to* . . .

A specific basis for comparison can be introduced in various ways — for example:

My car is the same colour as yours.

Our fridge is the same size as yours.

Our fridge is as big as yours.

Similarity of physical appearance can also be represented by a process:

Our fridge looks like yours.

Dewsbury looks like the prime minister.

Other processes can themselves be the basis of comparison:

He walks like his father does.

She swims like a fish.

He can run as fast as his brother.

Rebecca laughs like a witch.

When two things are presented as different, we often indicate the difference in terms of some specific dimension or attribute:

Our fridge is	older	than yours.
	taller	
	noisier	
	less efficient	
	better designed	
	more economical	
	more solidly built	

The structure of comparison

The structure we use for making the comparison is a phrase which includes *than*:

>   taller than   less efficient than

But what happens after the *than*? Let's take an example from the previous section:

>   Our fridge is noisier than yours.

This seems to be a single clause ending with the phrase *than yours*, which qualifies *noisier*; the word *than* operates like a preposition (a term discussed at the beginning of the next chapter). Yet the 'phrase' can be regarded as a shortened version of the clause *than yours is*, in which case *than* is clearly a conjunction introducing a second clause. This may be more obvious if we take the kind of example that traditional pedants would pounce on:

>   He is taller than me.

In this typical everyday usage we follow our instincts and end the sentence with *me*, in effect treating *than* as a preposition. The pedant would argue that the sentence is really short for *He is taller than I am*, where *than* introduces a little clause whose subject is *I*. That is why traditional teaching insisted on *He is taller than I*. In this kind of question, however, it's best to be aware of the options and follow your own preference.

   The adjective indicating the basis of the comparison can be brought into the noun group as an epithet. If the comparison is left implicit, *than . . .* can be omitted:

>   We need a bigger fridge (than the one we've got).

>   We'll have to get a more expensive fridge.

   For words indicating this kind of comparison, there are two distinct grammatical options. Some adjectives and a few adverbs have a special **comparative** form, which is written with the addition of the morpheme *-er* to the basic form. In speech the equivalent is an extra syllable, usually pronounced as the indefinite vowel $/ \mathrm{\partial} /$. Other adjectives and adverbs take the alternative option: the word *more* before the adjective or adverb. *Less* can be used in the same way, but it has no form equivalent to the *-er* ending. So we have:

happier	less happy	more happily	less happily
more efficient	less efficient	more efficiently	less efficiently

What governs the choice between the word *more* and the *-er* ending (i.e. between the syntactic and the morphological options)? The traditional teaching was that adjectives of one syllable take the *-er* ending, while almost all other adjectives (and adverbs) have *more*:

slow	slower	slowly	more slowly
careful	more careful	carefully	more carefully

Traditional teaching also recognised that some two-syllable adjectives take the *-er* ending: principally those ending in *-y* (but not adverbs ending in *-ly*, which take *more*) and those ending in *-le*. Here are some examples (which include the 'super' forms discussed in the next section):

easy	easier	easiest
happy	happier	happiest
simple	simpler	simplest
narrow	narrower	narrowest

However, actual usage in English is not as simple as traditional teaching makes it seem. There is a tendency for the *'more + adjective'* pattern to be used even when there is an *-er* form available. So we may find:

> more quiet   more easy   more simple
>
> The situation appeared to be growing daily more grave.
>
> Meat and milk supplies have been more scarce than usual.

This use of *more* is especially likely when there are two adjectives joined by *and*, only one of which has the *-er* option; the same applies to *most*:

> What could be more fair and reasonable than that?
>
> It was one of the most busy and congested parts of London.

According to traditional teaching, the last one should be:

> It was one of the busiest and most congested parts of London.

Super comparisons

Another kind of comparison is the one which puts something at the top of the charts for some particular quality. Rather than comparing two things, it's a way of saying that something has more of a certain quality than anything else — at least in a specific domain. This kind of comparison is traditionally known as the **superlative**:

> The line across the Nullarbor Plain is the longest stretch of straight railway line in the world.
>
> Jupiter is the largest planet in the solar system.
>
> Cape Byron is the most easterly point on the Australian mainland.
>
> For some years she had been the oldest surviving member of her family.

The forms available for this superlative comparison follow exactly the same pattern as the comparative forms (e.g. *easier, easiest; more mischievous, most mischievous*).

However, in most morphological aspects of grammar (i.e. those expressed in variations of the form of words), there some cases where the variations are irregular. The irregularities usually occur in very common words, as is evident in the comparison forms of adjectives and adverbs (i.e.

the -*er* and -*est* forms). Here are some well-known irregulars:

good well }	better	best	
bad badly }	worse	worst	
far {	further farther	furthest farthest	
old {	older elder	oldest eldest	*(general use)* *(family relationships)*
much	more	most	
little	less	least	

The last series applies only when *little* refers to quantity (i.e. *how little* of something, in contrast to *how much*) — not to size. When *little* refers to size, it can have the forms *littler* and *littlest* but they are mainly used by young children. Adults are more likely to use the comparison forms of *small* (i.e. *smaller* and *smallest*).

There is no clearly accepted distinction between *further* and *farther*, even though some try to claim that there is. In practice most people only use *further* and *furthest*, although *farther* and *farthest* can be found in some literary contexts.

Finally, it's worth noting here that the word *first* is a remnant of an old comparative series: *fore, former, first*. Expressions like *to the fore* and *first and foremost* hint at its origins.

Taking possession

Another way in which two things can be brought together is by means of a relationship broadly described as **possession**, or ownership — for example:

the woman's umbrella   my car   our school

While we call this relationship 'possession', it must be understood as a technical concept in grammar. Although it includes the general idea of ownership, it takes in much more than possession in the literal sense. The notion of possession is a metaphor in grammar for a wide range of relationships that can be expressed by the same grammatical resources.

There are several ways in which two things can be shown to be connected in this possessive relationship. The most basic is to use the possessive ending on the noun (the formal requirements for this will be set out shortly):

the women's choir   a boys' school

the story's main character   the team's new whip-cracking coach

Strictly speaking, the possessive ending is attached to the whole noun group, and not necessarily to the head noun, as these examples show:

> the king of Spain's daughter
>
> the archbishops of Canterbury and York's consultant on relations with other faiths

However, there is a strong tendency to drop the apostrophe in specific titles, partly from a desire for a neat, unfussy appearance in signs, letterheads and the like:

> Morpeth Girls High School the Ironworkers Union

Possession can also be shown by means of a phrase starting with a preposition (usually *of*):

> the daughter of the king of Spain the head of state
>
> the possessive form of the noun the mouth of the river

But sometimes prepositions other than *of* seem more appropriate:

> the main character in the story a school for boys

This variation in prepositions arises because several types of relationship are encompassed by the possessive form of nouns.

While the possessive noun and the prepositional phrase are essentially alternative ways of expressing the possessive relationship, one way often sounds better than the other in a particular instance — sometimes because it's a set phrase. For example:

> a dog's breakfast *not* the breakfast of a dog
>
> the team's new whip-cracking coach
> *rather than*
> the new whip-cracking coach of the team

On the other hand:

> the head of state *not* the state's head

Yet, like so many things in grammar, this is more a matter of judgement than of fixed rule. However, the judgement is often related to textual considerations, such as the need to emphasise a certain item by having it at the end of the group. And when there's a series of items related by possession, it's handy to be able to vary the means by which we express the relationship. Compare these sentences for example:

> The shop is run by one of Mrs Pearce's daughters' friends' parents.
>
> The shop is run by the parents of one of Mrs Pearce's daughters' friends.

The second is certainly easier to understand.

The possessive relationship can also be expressed as a process, and there are several verbs which allow us to do this:

> I've got five cents. The didgeridoo belongs to Jim.
>
> Do you own this land? He doesn't possess a dinner suit.

But these verbs don't always express literal ownership:

She's got a broken arm.   He's got blond hair and blue eyes.

The possessive forms of nouns in speech

In most nouns the possessive form is the same as the plural. That is, we add the sounds -/s/ or -/z/ or the syllable - /əz/, depending on the last sound of the basic form (see p. 59). So for most nouns the possessive form can only be distinguished from the basic plural form by the context; there is no audibly distinct possessive form. This means that in speech most nouns have only two forms: a basic form and an **inflected** (or marked) form. The inflected form means either plural or possessive or both — hence the ambiguity in speech of noun groups like *Mrs Pearces daughters friends parents* (apostrophes omitted).

It is only in nouns that have an irregular plural (e.g. *man, woman, child, tooth*) that the possessive form is audibly distinct. In these nouns the -/s/, -/z/ or - /əz/ endings mark only the possessive (not the plural) and the plural possessive is a distinctive form. So such nouns have four forms, a basic form and three inflected forms:

basic	possessive singular	basic plural	possessive plural
man	man's	men	men's

The possessive forms of nouns in writing

The possessive form is normally written by adding 's (apostrophe + s) to the basic singular or plural form. But if the basic form already ends in s, then we usually just add the apostrophe. This is *always* so in the plural, but in the singular an extra s may be added after the apostrophe. Consider these examples:

basic	possessive singular	basic plural	possessive plural
boy	boy's	boys	boys'
baby	baby's	babies	babies'
Ross	Ross's		
Xerxes	Xerxes'		
child	child's	children	children's
woman	woman's	women	women's

In most nouns the possessive forms are distinguished from the basic plural only by the apostrophe. *Boy* illustrates the most typical pattern.

The possessive forms of pronouns

Both the reference pronouns and speech role pronouns have possessive forms. Their use is similar to that of possessive nouns except that they mostly have two distinct forms, corresponding to these two positions of the possessive noun group:

That is John's guitar.	That guitar is John's.
That is my guitar.	That guitar is mine.

A possessive noun group like *John's* usually functions as a pointer in another noun group, as in the clause on the left; in this function the corresponding pronoun form is *my*. However, it is also possible for the possessive noun group to function as an independent attribute, as in the clause on the right. Possessive pronouns often function in this role too, but most have a special form for it, such as *mine*. For the other pronouns these forms are as follows:

your	yours	our	ours
his	his	their	theirs
her	hers	whose	whose
its	its	one's	–

Note that none of these possessive pronouns is written with an apostrophe, except for *one's*.

The apostrophe — problem or 'problem'?

It must be admitted that the conventions governing the use of the apostrophe in English are far from secure. There are at least two problems. One is that as the apostrophe has no counterpart in speech and we learn our language first through speech, many people are either uncertain or careless about its use. The second is that the -*s* (or -*es*) ending has several different roles in English and only some of them conventionally require the apostrophe. In particular, as we've just noted, possessive pronouns do not take apostrophes although possessive nouns do. That is one ground of confusion; the other is the use of the apostrophe to mark the small number of common English contractions, including *'s* to represent either *is* or *has*.

In much informal writing, then, and in some printed texts, the apostrophe is either not used at all or is used unconventionally. This suggests that the conventions may be breaking down and that the apostrophe may eventually disappear. Yet the basic conventions for using apostrophes are simple enough, and, like the conventions of spelling, they help to avoid ambiguity and ease the reader's passage through the text.

Apostrophes have two major functions in the written mode of the language:

1 They mark contractions, where letters have been omitted, especially in verb groups (e.g. *'s* for *is* or *has*, *'ll* for *will*, *hasn't* for *has not*, *won't* for *will not*.)

2 They distinguish the singular and plural possessive forms of the noun from the simple plural form.

(It may be helpful to mention here a hidden connection between these two functions: the possessive use of the apostrophe derives from a contraction of the old possessive form of the noun, which ended in -*es*.)

It follows that the apostrophe has no place in simple plurals (thus *Eggs for sale*, not *Egg's* or *Eggs' for sale*). Nor is there any need for it in abbreviations like *MPs* (*MP's*) or *1960s* (*1960's*).

Since the possessive forms of pronouns do not have the apostrophe (even those ending in -*s* like *his*, *its* or *theirs*), *it's* is left free to stand for the contractions of *it is* and *it has*.

Relationships in clauses and groups

In this chapter we've considered several relationships that can be expressed within the noun group. Some of them can also be expressed as a form of transitivity in clauses. For example, we saw in the last chapter that an attribute can be related to a thing either through a relational process or as an epithet in a noun group:

        This chair is comfortable.   This comfortable chair . . .

The same applies to possessives:

        John owns the guitar.   John's guitar . . .

Similar possibilities are available for comparisons:

        This piece is larger than that one.   This larger piece . . .

Here, however, the 'clause' can be described as two clauses, the second (*than that one*) having an implied verb *is*.

In exploring the resources of the noun group over the last two chapters, we have come to see how easily expandable and adaptable a structure it is. On many occasions we find it useful to be able to compress a clause into a noun group when we are expressing relationships that can be realised either way. But this is symptomatic of an increasing tendency for the noun group to encroach upon the territory of the verb group — a tendency which deserves a section to itself.

Nouning the verb

Noun groups, which enable us to represent all the things in our experience, typically function as participants in clauses; that is, they participate in some process. Yet, as we use language to construct our picture of the world, it's possible to talk about a process as if it were a thing — a feature of language use referred to as **nominalisation**. It allows us to change our viewpoint so that an activity is treated not as a process but as a thing presented in a noun group. Hence, 'nouning the verb'.

There are of course many words which can be used either as nouns or as verbs. Some common examples are *walk, talk, love, crash, change* and *increase*. Sometimes a verb is used as a noun but coupled with another verb to maintain a process, as in:

> *push*   to give someone a push
>
> *claim*   to make a claim
>
> *attack*   to mount an attack

Then there are other verbs which we sometimes press into the noun role when we say things like *Here, have a read of this*, or *It's a big ask.*

The *-ing* form of the verb is also used as a noun in many common expressions, such as:

> I have to do the washing.   Swimming is the best sport.

These are nominalisations in origin but are so well established in the language that we hardly think of them in that way. However, there are other much more ad hoc uses of *-ing* forms where the nominalisation is apparent. The verb form is used as the basis of a noun group — for example:

> One effect of global warming will be the melting of the polar ice caps.
>
> The riding of bicycles and the playing of ball games is prohibited in this park.

Another form of nominalisation is a clause based on the **infinitive** form of the verb (*to* + basic verb). But this is less common and rather formal:

> To err is human, to forgive divine.
>
> To say anything else might endanger the lives of the hostages.

One of the most common forms of nominalisation is a noun formed from a verb. Many verbs can be turned into abstract nouns. There are some interesting examples in this notice from a public hospital:

> FAILURE TO ATTEND FOR AN
> APPOINTMENT ON TWO SUCCESSIVE
> OCCASIONS, WITHOUT NOTIFICATION,
> WILL RENDER YOU INELIGIBLE
> FOR FURTHER TREATMENT.

We might try 'unpacking' this warning in two stages. First we can turn two nominalisations, *failure* and *notification*, back into verbs:

> If you fail to attend two successive appointments without notifying us, you will not be eligible for further treatment.

Then we can move this version closer to the everyday language of the people who might be affected:

> If you miss two appointments in a row without letting us know, you won't be able to get any more treatment.

Here is another example:

> Roses still bloom better in London than in remote country areas, a consequence of the destruction by the pollutant sulphur dioxide of the fungi which attack them.

The second part of the sentence consists of a post-modified noun group based on *consequence*, which can be compared with the implied clause *because the pollutant sulphur dioxide destroys the fungi which attack them*. The key to the structure is the nominalisation of the process *destroys*.

Nominalisation may be thought of as using a noun derived from a verb to make a thing out of a process. However, as the last example shows, there is more to it than that. A process is at the heart of a clause, and the process disappears if the clause is packaged as a noun group. The result is often a concentration of meaning in the noun group which requires some unpacking on the part of the listener or reader — an operation that may be especially challenging for a young reader.

Here are unpacked versions of two of the earlier examples:

> When the globe warms up, one effect will be that the polar ice caps will melt.

> You must not ride bicycles or play ball games in this park.

These versions realise the clauses implied in the original examples, making process and agent explicit. However, going the other way round and converting a clause into a noun group can sometimes blur the transitivity that is clear in the original clause and lead to ambiguity — as in this example from an animal liberationist speaking about circus animals:

> These animals are forced to perform night after night for the purpose of enjoyment. (*cf.* so that the spectators can enjoy themselves)

Nominalisations tend to present experience in a very compact way, and this is often an advantage in formal written texts. Moreover, the nominalisation can easily be modified by an epithet:

> the gradual undermining of their position

> make that important decision

Nominalisation is undoubtedly a very useful resource and yet, like all good things, one can have too much of it. The density of a text which relies heavily on nominalisation can make it inaccessible to all but a specialist audience. Sometimes, especially in bureaucratic, legal and technical fields, one may suspect that this is part of the intention. After all, language can be used to exert authority or intimidate, to exclude as well as to include.

In the Circumstances

In the previous three chapters we have explored the ways in which two functional components of clauses (*processes* and *participants*) help us to make a detailed representation of our experience of the world. We have considered how verb groups realise processes (Chapter 5) and how we make reference to things by means of noun groups, which often function as participants in clauses (Chapters 6 and 7). The third functional component of the clause indicates the *circumstances* in which these processes and participants operate. The most common circumstances are time and place; others include manner and reason.

Circumstances can be expressed in various ways. Earlier (on p. 19) we noted that where a circumstance is a component of a clause, there is some variety in the grammatical structures that can express it: for example, a single word, a noun group or a phrase. Sometimes, too, a circumstance needs a clause of its own — something we'll deal with in the next chapter. In this chapter we'll consider circumstances realised as components of the clause and some of the other ways in which they can be expressed — for instance, through the grammar of the verb group (time) and by lexical means (manner).

The most common structure for representing a circumstance is the **prepositional phrase**, so called because it is typically introduced by a **preposition** — one of a small class of words (such as *on, at, in, to, from*) which indicate particular relationships. The phrase normally consists of a preposition followed by a noun group:

in	1994
over	the weekend
over	the moon
on	the mat
after	Christmas
with	no strings attached
preposition	noun group

Circumstances can also be expressed by **adverbs** or **adverbial groups** (that is, a word group based on an adverb). Adverbs are a class of words used for expressing not only circumstances but some other meanings too, such as modality (e.g. *probably*), speaker's attitude (e.g. *unfortunately*) and textual connections (e.g. *consequently*). Many adverbs, but by no means all, end in *-ly*. Adverbial groups include such modified expressions as *very skilfully*, *much too quickly* and *almost certainly*.

Marking time

Time plays such an important part in our representation of experience that there are more grammatical resources for expressing it than there are for other circumstances. They include:

- the verb group (different structures and forms)
- adverbial expressions (single words, phrases and clauses).

There are three basic divisions of time: past, present and future. In speech these are usually expressed from the speaker's time viewpoint (writing is more variable):

– *looking back to the past:*

   She arrived a couple of hours ago.

– *concurrent with the time of speaking:*

   The film's just starting.

– *looking forward to the future:*

   They're getting married in two weeks' time.

It's also possible, both in speech and writing, to have 'timeless' messages, such as general principles or statements of general practice which apply at any time:

   Roses are red; violets are blue.

   Oil floats on water.

   I like my coffee black with one sugar.

Other points of origin for time orientation are possible too:

   Next year we will have been living in this house for ten years.

   They had left before we even arrived.

In the first example, the speaker is saying what it will be like to look back on the past when 'we' get to some point in the future. In the second, the speaker looks at the past from a point already in the past; it is a view of the past involving two stages — what Huddleston (1988, p. 77) calls 'a double dose of pastness'.

We can also indicate circumstances of time by referring to a conventional scale of dates or times, as in phrases like:

   in 1984   at 2.30   since 12 June

or by reference to the cycle of the seasons:

> last summer   after the winter

However, we often make time references in relation to other events. Because these events are typically quite specific, they usually need a full clause to specify them — for example:

> Just after my husband left me I won the lottery.
>
> I'll feed the chooks while you're getting the breakfast.
>
> Don't forget to clean your teeth before you go to bed.

We can also indicate the length of time that something takes (i.e. duration) with either a phrase or a clause:

> We lived there for thirty years.
>
> Keep an eye on the fire till I come back.
>
> He's been out all day.

Frequency is another option:

> That happens two or three times a day.
>
> Do you come here often?

Time, place and movement

Time and place are often closely connected, both in meaning and in the words used to express them. This is especially so when movement is involved, but not only then. A simple word like *before*, usually a matter of time, can also — somewhat formally now — refer to place:

> He took his place before the assembled crowd.

Two people arguing about who was *before* the other in a queue are disputing both place and time. As for place, time and motion, compare these directions:

> It's the first street on the left after the bank.
>
> Take the first turn on the left after you pass the bank.

The sense of motion made explicit in the second example is implicit in the first.

Time and tense

The time reference of any message is expressed in a general way by the verb group; time is closely bound up with the process. The term *tense* has traditionally been used to refer to the variant forms of the verb group associated with time. However, there is no simple parallel between time settings (such as past, present and future) and the tense forms of the English verb group.

The verb group has both simple forms (i.e. one word) and compound forms (more than one word). A variation between two simple forms of the verb allows us to make a basic distinction between 'past' and 'anything that is not past'. At this simple level we may say that there are only two tenses in English:

past: the time setting for narrative (accounts of experience, stories and so on) and for recounts of what has been done or what has happened

non-past: the time setting for everything else — running commentary, description, reports on how things are, generalisation, theory, speculation, prediction, etc.

The meaning of 'past' is easier to describe because it is more specific. The 'non-past' element is essentially just a way into a number of further distinctions, which we'll come to in a moment. But first we must consider the way these meanings are expressed in the verb forms.

Past forms

In the basic variation of the verb form, the past is the marked tense — the meaning that has a special form of its own. With one important exception, the non-past is unmarked; it uses the basic form of the verb.

Most verbs in English form their past tense according to a regular pattern, but there are a number of common verbs which are irregular. The written form of the regular pattern has -*ed* or -*d* added to the basic verb form:

non-past	walk	smile	wait
past	walked	smiled	waited

In speech, the basic form has the sounds /t/, /d/ or /əd/ added (depending on the final sound of the basic form). The examples above represent each of the three types.

There are various irregular verbs which add -*t* (sometimes with a vowel change as well):

learn	spell	dream	leave	catch
learnt	spelt	dreamt	left	caught

Note, however, that *learn*, *spell* and *dream* can also form a regular -*ed* past tense.

Then there are some verbs which make no change (i.e. their past tense is not formally marked). The basic forms of all these verbs end in -*t* or -*d*:

put	cost	shut	shed
put	cost	shut	shed

But most common irregular verbs form their past tense by changing the vowel:

feed	find	get	take	know	swim	lead	read
fed	found	got	took	knew	swam	led	read

Note that for *read* the change is only apparent in the spoken form.

Non-past forms

The non-past meanings are indicated by two forms of the verb:

- the basic or unmarked form
- a marked form ending in -s or -es.

This variation is illustrated by the following pairs:

look	boil	drive	wish	go	do	have
looks	boils	drives	wishes	goes	does	has

The lower one of each pair is formed in the same way as the plural of nouns, except for a few irregulars like *has*. Yet even though this marked form looks like a plural noun, it is a singular verb. Here is a formal paradox in English: a singular noun subject has a verb which looks like a plural noun and vice versa. Compare:

> The tiger feeds on other animals.   *(singular subject and verb)*
>
> Tigers feed on other animals.   *(plural subject and verb)*

The traditional explanation for the use of this marked form of the verb is that it goes with a 'third person singular' subject (for 'persons', see pp. 26–27). In other words, it is the form which follows *he, she, it* or virtually any other singular subject except the first and second person pronouns *I* and *you*.

However, while the idea of 'person' may be useful for describing the differences between pronouns (*I, you, he,* etc.), it has little relevance for verb forms in English. The only verb in present-day English which has different non-past forms for first, second and third persons is the verb *be* and then only in the singular (the forms *am, are* and *is* respectively). The one plural non-past form is *are*.

A more useful explanation recognises the distinction between speech role pronouns like *I* and *you* and reference pronouns like *he, she* and *it* which emerged in Chapter 3. The key is the reference function shared by reference pronouns and all other noun group subjects except for the speech role pronouns. We can say that a non-past verb will have the marked form if its subject is singular, unless it is a speech role pronoun.

The non-past forms are available for several meanings, which are either evident from the context or can be specified by a circumstance within the clause. Here are some examples:

generalisation:	Water boils at 100° Celsius.
description:	Bennelong Point juts out into the harbour.
commentary:	Hunt now bowls to Fox . . . he pushes out into the covers where the ball's picked up by O'Brien.
prediction:	The plane leaves at 3.00 pm.
intention:	We go on Tuesday.

Other aspects of the verb group

In addition to the basic past/non-past distinction, there is a range of other meanings which can be expressed by various auxiliary verbs in combination with different forms of the main verb. In such verb groups incorporating an auxiliary, the past/non-past distinction is expressed through the first auxiliary.

Progressive forms (be + -ing)

The **progressive** form of the verb group consists of an auxiliary (the verb *be*) together with the *-ing* form of the main verb (e.g. *cooking*). This form is known as the **present participle** and all verbs follow the same pattern (i.e. there are no irregularities). The auxiliary *be* comes in the usual forms (*am, is, are, was, were*, etc.).

Essentially the progressive form indicates that the process is continuing:

The peas are boiling over.   Interest rates are rising.

Yet for many verbs, especially action verbs, this non-past progressive is the true present tense, the one which indicates a present event. The simple non-past tense of these verbs is concerned with generalisation, as can be seen in these two contrasting examples:

He drinks coffee with milk and sugar.

He is [*or* He's] drinking his third cup of coffee.

However, there are many verbs, especially mental process verbs, which don't normally use the *be + -ing* structure. They use the basic form even for present reference:

I know the best thing to do.   (*not*   I am knowing . . .)

They believe we can go tomorrow.   (*not*   They are believing . . .)

The *be + -ing* structure can also be used to refer to a past happening; again it carries the idea of a continuing process:

He was drinking his third cup of coffee.

Still more meanings can be expressed by combining the *-ing* form with other auxiliaries:

He may be coming with us.   (*modality*)

I will [*or* I'll] be working late tonight.   (*modulation*)

Perfect forms (have + -ed)

Further nuances of meaning can be expressed by a verb group formed by combining the auxiliary *have* (including *has* and *had*) with a main verb. The form of the main verb which combines with *have* is the *past participle*, introduced in Chapter 5. In regular verbs it is the same as the past tense form (i.e. it ends in *-ed*) but in many irregular verbs it has a different form (see p. 52).

This combination of *have* with the past participle is traditionally known as the *perfect tense*. However, as the term *tense* is best used for the past/non-past distinction, this combination can simply be referred to as the **perfect** form of the verb group. Its meaning is best approached through some examples:

> She has [*or* She's] washed the car.
>
> You have [*or* You've] done a good job.

Both these statements clearly refer to something that has already happened but neither consigns it to the past in quite the same way that the past tense does. Now compare two more examples:

> She has just washed the car.
>
> She washed the car last weekend.

The perfect form (*has washed*) seems to have some connection with the present; it's the sort of remark that might be addressed to someone waiting for 'her'. But the past tense (*washed*) isolates the event in the past and there's an end of the matter — even if it's the very recent past, as in:

> She washed the car only this morning.

Thus the perfect form (*has washed*, etc.) may be said to straddle the past and the present; it can be regarded as past with a continuing relevance in the present. However, it can be shifted further into the past by using the past tense form of *have* (i.e. *had*), which is known as the **past perfect** or **pluperfect** form:

> She had washed the car by the time I arrived.

This can be compared with a version slanted towards the future:

> She will have washed the car by the time I arrive.

A note on contractions

Contraction can affect both the perfect and progressive forms, for the auxiliary is often unstressed in speech and so can be contracted. Such contractions are also used in informal writing, as in these examples:

> I'm washing the car.
>
> I've washed the car.
>
> She's [*i.e.* She is] washing the car.
>
> She's [*i.e.* She has] washed the car.

Note that the last two contractions are distinguished only by the form of the main verb, though the broader context may also help to clarify the distinction.

Confusion sometimes arises about the spelling of contractions simply because they aren't recognised for what they are. When people who are uncertain of the verb system write down contracted forms that they're familiar with in speech, they are quite likely to produce misspellings like these:

> Your washing the car.   She should of washed the car.

Your and *you're* are not clearly distinguished in pronunciation, and the same is true of *should've* and *should of* as long as the last element is unstressed, which it normally is. So the pronunciation is no guide to the spelling; some understanding of the verb system is necessary.

Multiple contractions are also possible when more than one auxiliary or a negative is involved. Here are two examples which, like the last one discussed, involve modal auxiliaries with the perfect *have*:

> I'd've washed the car if I'd known you were coming.
>
> I couldn't've taken the car as I'd lost the key.

However, while multiple contractions may be readily used in speech, they are much less common in writing, where they look awkward.

Modal auxiliaries

The modal auxiliaries introduced in Chapter 4 can also be used to express meanings related to time, especially future time, but they often carry other components of meaning as well. You will recall that the main ones are:

> shall   will   can   may   must
>
> should   would   could   might

The modals do not have a special -*s* form for third person singular, but the first four do have a kind of past tense in the forms on the second line. Here are some examples of their use, all looking towards the future:

> It could rain.   You should do something about this.
>
> I must go.   The end will come.

It is also possible to express other variations of meaning with combinations of modal, perfect and progressive auxiliaries, as in these examples:

> She will have washed the car.
>
> She could have washed the car.
>
> She should have washed the car.
>
> She would have washed the car, but . . .
>
> She must have washed the car, judging from the look of it.
>
> She has been washing the car.
>
> She ought to have been washing the car.

Whatever the combination, the order of auxiliaries is always this: modal, perfect, progressive. There can be only one modal unless they are co-ordinated with *and* — for example, *There can and must be only one modal* (which is strictly speaking two verb groups).

Time words and structures

We have just seen that there are many possible variations to the verb group which enable us to express a number of different time references and shades of meaning related to time. But these meanings are not nearly as specific as those that we can express as circumstances, which we rely on for all the fine details of reference to time, duration and frequency.

Such expressions include some single-word adverbs, like:

yesterday	today	tomorrow
now	later	simultaneously
before	afterwards	
seldom	often	
occasionally	frequently	

However, it is word groups, phrases and clauses which provide the most extensive resources for time reference. Here are some examples:

last night	a minute ago
before midnight	six years ago
at 2.30 pm	next Sunday
the day before yesterday	on the second Sunday of the month

and the infamous cliché:

at this point in time

There are also indications of duration:

all the morning	for two hundred years
until lunchtime	from 9 to 5

and frequency:

every Friday	once a month
every five minutes	once in a blue moon

Time clauses are mainly those which start with words like *when, while* and *before*. We'll deal with them in the next chapter.

A place for everything

Ever since the first cat sat on the first mat we have been putting people (and things) in their places. Even though it's usually not essential to indicate the location of the things and processes we are speaking or writing about, we very often do. Indeed, apart from time (and some sort of time reference is virtually unavoidable because it's built into the verb group), place is the most common circumstance we choose to express.

Some of our references to place make use of one or other of two systems of spatial orientation available to us. One is the relative system, *left* and *right*, based on our own body orientation, which is made explicit in *the left-*

hand side and *the right-hand side*. The other, based on the directions *north*, *south*, *east* and *west*, is more of an absolute system (as long as we don't stray too near the poles or out into space). In English we tend to use it for large-scale geographical relationships rather than for our immediate environment, though this is not so in all cultures. The conventional order in which we name the compass points doesn't run clockwise but suggests two sub-systems, *north–south* and *east–west* — axial relationships which are hinted at in the forms of the words themselves.

Another general way of indicating place is with the words *here* and *there*, meaning relatively close to or distant from the speaker's position. There's also the handy little group of words based on *where*: *everywhere, somewhere, elsewhere, anywhere* and *nowhere*.

However, by far the most common way of indicating place is the fairly specific phrase which relates what we are talking about to a particular thing, as in (dare I repeat it?):

> The cat sat on the mat.

We can indicate location both for static processes and for processes implying movement, as this bit of folklore suggests:

> The cow jumped over the moon.

Quite a number of examples are to be found in the following text, and you might like to complete the list appended below:

> I advanced alone to the centre of the town by the simple expedient of knocking on people's doors . . . The good burghers of Maidstone . . . let me through their houses and into their gardens. Here I would climb into a neighbouring garden, and knock on the back door of another house. These people would then let me out of their front doors. Looking both ways, I would then race across the road and knock at another front door, and the process would repeat itself.
>
> (Peter Ustinov, *Dear Me*)

| to the centre of the town | on people's doors |
| through their houses | into a neighbouring garden |

Location can be specified more precisely by a series of phrases, each amplifying the context for the preceding one.

> at a shop in the city
> on the top shelf behind the stuffed wombat
> along Sutter Street in San Francisco . . . close to the usually safe Japantown

Another structure used for putting things in their place is the clause. Such clauses usually start with *where* or *wherever*:

> This is the spot where the Vinegar Hill tragedy occurred.
> Put it wherever you can find a spot for it.

The following passage illustrates several types of expression for indicating location — single words, phrases and clauses:

> Fog everywhere. Fog up the river, where it flows among green aits and meadows; fog down the river, where it rolls defiled among the tiers of shipping, and the waterside pollutions of a great (and dirty) city. Fog on the Essex marshes, fog on the Kentish heights. Fog creeping into the cabooses of collier-brigs; fog lying out on the yards and hovering in the rigging of great ships; fog drooping on the gunwales of barges and small boats. Fog in the eyes and throats of ancient Greenwich pensioners, wheezing by the firesides of their wards; fog in the stem and bowl of the afternoon pipe of the wrathful skipper; fog cruelly pinching the toes and fingers of his shivering little 'prentice boy on deck. Chance people on the bridges peeping over the parapets into a nether sky of fog, with fog all round them, as if they were up in a balloon, and hanging in the misty clouds.
>
> (Charles Dickens, *Bleak House*)

The manner of the doing

Recipes and other procedures are full of instructions about how to do things:

> Measure carefully . . .
>
> Divide evenly . . .
>
> Whisk lightly with a fork . . .
>
> Start to cook slowly . . .
>
> Stir gently with a wooden spoon . . .
>
> Carefully cut along the dotted line.
>
> Clamp firmly until the glue is set.

The single words for indicating the manner in which such things are done, like *carefully*, *lightly*, *slowly* and *gently*, are typical adverbs. Most are formally related to descriptive adjectives, and the language offers us a rich supply of them. This means that we are not so dependent on phrases and clauses for conveying the circumstance of manner as we are for time and place. Nevertheless it is possible to use a phrase or a clause rather than an adverb, though the result may seem unnecessarily wordy — as here:

> Cut along the dotted line in a careful way.

On the other hand, the slight emphasis gained by placing a phrase of manner at the end of this road sign seems entirely appropriate:

> Turn left at any time with care.

There is another lexical resource which allows us to convey some idea of how something is done. Many processes can be referred to either by a general word which does not itself specify how the process was done, or by a more specific word which implies a particular manner of doing. For example, take a simple everyday action like *walk*. That word implies nothing about the manner of the walking, but many other words do: for instance, *amble, saunter, stroll, strut, stride, march*. Any thesaurus will provide you with more variants. Here then is further evidence of the lexical richness of the language in this area of meaning: the manner of a process can often be indicated by the verb itself. It confirms that we are less dependent on syntactic resources in the form of phrases — let alone full clauses of manner (e.g. those beginning with *how*). Yet these resources are available if needed.

Other circumstances

There are other circumstances which can be represented in the clause by means of a prepositional phrase. They include the following:

reason:	because of, as a result of, thanks to The sports day was postponed because of the rain.
purpose:	for, for the purpose of They would often meet for dinner.
behalf:	for the sake of, on behalf of I am speaking on behalf of the staff.
accompaniment:	*(positive)* with, besides I went to the beach with my Nanna and Grandad. *(negative)* without, instead of They left without food or money.
matter:	about They were talking about the proposed freeway.
role:	as I want to give you some advice as a friend.

However, for some circumstances, including time, place and reason, a full clause is often needed. This will be dealt with in Chapter 9.

Links with traditional grammar

While traditional grammar uses terms like *preposition* and *phrase*, it does not recognise the prepositional phrase as a structure. Prepositional phrases are known as *adverbial phrases* and *adjectival phrases*, which are identified on the basis of their functions. Thus a prepositional phrase denoting place would traditionally be called an *adverbial phrase of place*; one functioning as a post-modifier in a noun group (e.g. *the last one in the row*) would be called an *adjectival phrase*. It might appear that in using the term *prepositional phrase* we are ignoring a functional distinction which traditional grammar recognises. In fact we are making the functional distinction in other terms (circumstance: location – post-modifier) and at the same time identifying a structure for which traditional grammar has no single term.

Complex Messages

Clauses and sentences

Inevitably we've already said a great deal about clauses because they play such an important part in the expression of meaning. And we've seen how any clause by itself expresses a simple message. However, we often want to expand the basic message by putting more than one clause together in the one sentence. Thus we get a more complex message.

Let's imagine that we want to compose a whole text involving a number of ideas. We might try writing it out as a series of simple sentences, one clause (i.e. one message) in each. But we'd soon find that this approach prevents us showing how some clauses are closely related to others and that it reduces the overall fluency and cohesion of the text. So, in reality, we are much more likely to group two or more clauses together in one sentence to express expanded, more complex messages.

To illustrate the point, we'll first break down a short complex text. Then we'll examine expanded messages more systematically.

TEXT 9.1 AN EXTRACT FROM A RADIO NEWS BROADCAST

Many of the Cambodians on the Indonesian refugee-holding island of Galang, who have fled Cambodia by boat and who intend to come to Australia, are young men who have left because they want to avoid conscription for military service and because they are generally fed up with the war and poor conditions.

This long sentence, consisting of six clauses, brings several messages together in a complex of relationships. If we try expressing them as a series of separate sentences, what happens?

> Many of the Cambodians on the Indonesian refugee-holding island of Galang are young men.
>
> They have fled Cambodia by boat.
>
> They intend to come to Australia.
>
> The young men have left Cambodia.
>
> They want to avoid conscription for military service.
>
> They are generally fed up with the war and poor conditions.

Such a version conveys most of the meaning of the original, but it doesn't show all the relationships between the messages, nor does it read as fluently. Admittedly it would be possible to combine some of the sentences without necessarily putting them all together in the one sentence, as Text 9.1 does. Equally, however, we could go further the other way and break them down into even simpler grammatical structures — for instance, by having more clauses with simpler noun groups. The first sentence will serve as an example:

> Cambodian refugees are held on the Indonesian island of Galang.
>
> Many of them are young men.

There are in fact many different ways in which a group of ideas can be presented using the grammatical resources that English offers us. Any particular option will tend to emphasise certain relationships and thus will differ slightly in meaning from other options. Nevertheless, in this chapter and the next, we'll be concerned mainly with possibilities at the level of clauses and sentences rather than at the level of noun groups or other structures within the clause.

Parallel clauses

When we have a series of clauses representing a series of connected messages, some of them can be linked together in the one sentence by means of conjunctions like *and* or *but*. Even though the conjunction signifies some connection between them (perhaps one of time or relevance to the topic), the clauses still retain their independent status. Thus we can refer to them as **parallel** clauses. We'll look at some examples drawn from two broadcast accounts of a plane crash.

> TEXT 9.2 AN EXTRACT FROM A RADIO NEWS BULLETIN (i.e. read from a script)
>
> An official investigation has begun into this morning's crash of a light plane at Mt Bindo, near Oberon, west of Katoomba. Four people were on board the Cessna 177, which crashed after it lost power. They all escaped serious injury. They were the pilot [and three other young men from Sydney]. Police said the four left from Hoxton Park and over Mt Bindo the aircraft lost power. The pilot tried to land on a small airstrip in a clearing but the aircraft struck some pine trees and crashed. The occupants jumped clear as it burst into flames. Although the crash occurred in rugged terrain, it was witnessed by off-road enthusiast Brian Cotwell.

TEXT 9.3 EYE-WITNESS ACCOUNT OF THE CRASH (broadcast from a tape)

He circled us first and then he was going to come back just to . . . straight down the airstrip just to have a look before he . . . landed. He came up along the airstrip and he tried coming up over these trees here and er . . . he started lifting up and then he just sort of suddenly started dropping . . . and then the plane just tilted over to one side and just started collecting all these trees and then it just hit there . . . and er . . . when we got up here it was just all . . . it was only just the front of it burning, you know, but er . . . they'd already got out and one fellow had already walked off up the road and I think he was in a bit of a daze, you know.

In both these texts we have examples of clauses joined by *and* indicating a time sequence:

> . . . the four left from Hoxton Park and over Mt Bindo the aircraft lost power.

> He came up along the airstrip and he tried coming up over these trees here and he started lifting up and then he just sort of suddenly started dropping and then the plane just tilted over to one side and just started collecting all these trees and then it just hit there . . .

A series of clauses joined by *and* or *and then* (as in the last example) is quite a common way of giving on oral account of a series of events occurring one after the other. It's also very common in children's early writing where a series of events is being described, as in this example:

> One day we went to Gosford and we went fishing there and I caught two tailor and we ate them and we went to Woy Woy and I caught a fish there and I caught the fish with a rod.

As noted earlier, it's possible for parallel clauses to be joined by *but*:

> The pilot tried to land on a small air strip in a clearing
> but the aircraft struck some pine trees and crashed.

There are in fact three parallel clauses here, but the second and third share the same subject (*the aircraft* — understood before *crashed*) and are joined by *and*. Thus the preceding *but* applies to both of them and shows that both stand in contrast to the first clause (*The pilot tried to land . . . but . . .*).

However, *and* and *but* are not the only means of linking parallel clauses. The main types of relationship that can be established between them and the means of indicating these relationships can be summarised as follows:

addition:	and
marked addition:	not only . . . but also
contrast:	but
alternatives:	either . . . or, neither . . . nor
time sequence:	then

reason: for

consequence: and so (*informal* so)

Here are some examples of types of parallel clause not yet illustrated:

> *Not only* is that a ridiculous suggestion, *but* it could *also* land you in real trouble.

> We'll *either* go today *or* put it off till next week.

> Josh arrived, *then* there was a sudden storm and we all had to dash inside.

> After two hours he had to halt the advance, *for* the scouts had not yet returned.

> Some of the singers had laryngitis *and so* the concert had to be cancelled.

Parallel clauses can also be linked within the sentence by a semi-colon. This usually implies that the second clause is some kind of elaboration or extension of the first — for example:

> There hasn't been a single case of smallpox for over ten years on the entire planet; it's considered extinct.

Even though parallel clauses are of equal status, the order in which they occur is important. The order is part of the meaning. The first clause initiates something which is continued in the second — and sometimes in subsequent clauses. However, where there is a series of continuing clauses notionally joined by *and*, the *and* need appear only before the last clause in the series; the rest are separated by commas. Here's an example adapted from Text 9.4 :

> Margaret climbed onto the table, Alexander dived under it, Richard raced after the headless snake and their mother stood very still.

In the case of marked addition and alternatives, the initiating clause may also be introduced by a conjunction (*not only, either/neither*).

Before we go any further, we should familiarise ourselves with the text from which the last example is derived.

TEXT 9.4 AN EXTRACT FROM A CHILDREN'S NOVEL

Even on such a hot night, the baked rabbit and vegetables were tasty. They ate in silence while the insects smacked into the light on the wall and the mosquitoes added more polka dots to their bare arms and legs.

Jennifer gazed out into the darkness, swallowing with difficulty the rhubarb pie and cream. There were two things she hated: Linda Grey and rhubarb. The other children knew she hated it, and enjoyed watching her as she washed it down with great gulps of water.

She was so engrossed in her battle with the rhubarb that she did not notice her mother leaving the table, nor her return, until she saw shock on the faces of Richard and Margaret.

Spinning around, she saw her mother pointing the shotgun at the honeysuckle wall, and, following the direction of the gun, glimpsed with horror the coiled body of a snake entwined there.

The blast of the gun scattered the children from the table. They fell over each other and their chairs while the decapitated snake did a quick one-way trip along the verandah.

Everything with ears shrieked or barked or shrilled or mooed. Margaret climbed onto the table, Alexander dived under it, Richard raced after the headless snake with his chair poised over his head, and their mother, white-faced and calm, stood very still, as though she were in the habit of taking pot shots at snakes during dessert.

(Thurley Fowler, *The Green Wind*)

A hierarchy of clauses

In many sentences made up of two clauses, one clause provides the main message and the other modifies it, introducing some extra information which has a bearing on the main message. Unless the clauses are parallel and separated by a semi-colon, the clause giving extra information is said to be **dependent** on the clause with the main message — that is, each clause has a different status. Examples from Text 9.2 are:

The occupants jumped clear as it burst into flames.

Although the crash occurred in rugged terrain, it was witnessed by off-road enthusiast Brian Cotwell.

In the first example, *the occupants jumped clear* is presented as the main message; *as it burst into flames* is offered as an additional piece of information, expanding the basic message. In the second example the dependent clause comes first, preparing the reader for the basic message.

It's perfectly possible to have a series of dependent clauses in the one sentence, each except the main clause being dependent on another — as in the examples below, where the hierarchy of the clauses is marked alphabetically:

A Four people were on board the Cessna 177

B   which crashed

C   after it lost power.

This example may be contrasted with the second sentence from Text 9.4, which also contains three clauses, representing three activities going on at the same time. But two of them (marked B1 and B2) are of equal status (i.e. parallel clauses) and both are dependent on the main clause:

A They ate in silence

B1   while the insects smacked into the light on the wall

B2   and the mosquitoes added more polka dots to their bare arms and legs.

Another example (from Text 1.2) shows the parallel dependent clauses coming first:

> B1   If they're cut open
>
> B2   and I take the pulp out of them now,
>
> A   they'll probably be all right.

We'll now consider the meaning of some of the dependent relationships that can exist between clauses.

Additional information

A dependent clause may be used simply to bring in pertinent information to supplement the message of the main clause. Examples from Text 9.1 are:

> who have fled Cambodia by boat
>
> and who intend to come to Australia

Although the additional information is usually linked to a particular noun group in the main clause (in this case, *Many of the Cambodians on the Indonesian refugee-holding island of Galang*), it can be presented as an elaboration on the whole clause, as in this example:

> The Cambodians were held on the island of Galang, which was not what they wanted.

These clauses of additional information are known as **relative** clauses. They usually begin with one of the WH words *who, whom, which* or *whose* (i.e. relative pronouns). Relative clauses can also be used for a different function, which we'll come to when we look at 'embedded' clauses later in the chapter.

Time and place

As we noted in the previous chapter, relationships of time are often expressed through dependent clauses. They are typically introduced by time conjunctions, such as:

> when   whenever   as   while
>
> before   after   until   since

> He had touched it before I was able to warn him.
>
> When the roll is called up yonder, I'll be there.
>
> After the dust settles we'll be able to see what the damage is.
>
> This was the first time it had happened since we came to town.

Clauses indicating place are not as common as time clauses. They are usually introduced by the conjunctions *where* and *wherever*:

> She shall have music wherever she goes.

Two simultaneous events can be indicated by a time clause beginning with *while*, as in this example from Text 9.4:

> They fell over each other and their chairs while the decapitated snake did a quick one-way trip along the verandah.

It would be possible to reverse the order of the clauses in this way:

> The decapitated snake did a quick one-way trip along the verandah while they fell over each other and their chairs.

However, although the meaning would be much the same, the connection with the previous sentence would be impaired. Starting the sentence with the *while* clause would similarly affect the emphasis and the development of meaning in the whole passage.

Logical relationships
In order to show relationships like causes or conditions, we often use clauses introduced by conjunctions that specify the particular relationship. Some of the main relationships and their associated conjunctions are set out with examples below:

reason:	because, since, as He won't agree because he'd lose face.
purpose:	so that, in order that Turn it off so that you don't get distracted.
result:	so . . . that She was so engrossed in her battle with the rhubarb that she did not notice her mother leaving the table.
condition:	if, unless If we come, we'll have to bring the dog.
concession:	although, though, even if, even though Although I don't want to, I suppose I'll have to agree.
comparison:	as, as if, as though and their mother stood very still, as though she were in the habit of taking pot shots at snakes during dessert.

In some contexts it may be necessary to make the relationship very explicit by introducing the clause with a more complex conjunction, such as:

> for the reason that   on condition that   until such time as

A note on since and as
These two conjunctions can be used for relationships of both time and reason, as these pairs of examples demonstrate:

> We've lived here since my aunt died.
> We stay here, since we can't afford to move.

> As we ran out of petrol the car spluttered to a standstill.
> As we had run out of petrol, we locked the car and started walking.

Usually the context or the verb tenses make it clear which relationship is intended, but occasionally there can be a touch of ambiguity, as in this example from Text 5.1:

> I made eye contact with one of them, as he was trying to attract my attention by wild gesticulation.

Note that *as* can also be used for other relationships, such as manner:

> We'll do it the same way as we always have.

Other possibilities

The relationships outlined above can sometimes be expressed in other ways, using a variety of grammatical resources. For example, a condition can be expressed by adopting the interrogative word order:

> Should you require any further assistance, don't hesitate to ring.

Sometimes a clause can be replaced by a phrase:

> Even though he was ill, he still won the race.
> Despite his illness, he still won the race.

Internal and external

It's not unusual to find sentences where the clause relationship appears to involve false logic. Consider these examples:

> If you are a grazier living in the southern highlands of NSW, we have a sheep weather alert.   (radio broadcast)
> If you look closely, one of them's broken.
> There's a swimming pool here if you want to cool off.

At first sight the *if* clauses seem to involve conditions which aren't genuine — for instance, the swimming pool must be there whether anyone wants to swim in it or not. Yet the conditions are real enough; it's just that they apply to something not stated, something taken for granted. Let's try filling out what's implied:

> If you are a grazier living in the southern highlands of NSW, you'll be interested to know that we have a sheep weather alert.
> If you look closely, you'll see that one of them's broken.
> There's a swimming pool here; I'm telling you this in case you want to cool off.

Clauses like these are called internal conditions, because they are conditions applying to the discourse itself rather than the external world that the discourse is referring to. Here's another example which contains an internal cause rather than a condition:

> She's definitely coming because she told me yesterday.
> (She's definitely coming; I know that because she told me yesterday.)

Non-finite clauses

Some of the relationships that can be expressed in terms of the clause hierarchies we've been examining can also be suggested by means of non-finite clauses. The typical clause is **finite** — that is, as we saw in Chapter 3, it has its own subject and its own finite element: a first auxiliary or a simple main verb which carries the tense. However, it's quite possible to have a clause without these elements. It is called a **non-finite** clause and will normally be attached to another clause, one of whose participants will serve as its implicit subject.

In this sentence from Text 9.4 there are several examples of non-finite clauses:

> Spinning around, she saw her mother pointing the shotgun at the honeysuckle wall, and, following the direction of the gun, glimpsed with horror the coiled body of a snake entwined there.

The first finite clause is *she saw her mother*, but this has two non-finite clauses associated with it. The first one, *spinning around*, has the same subject as the finite clause. We can see the relationship involved if we change the order and insert the non-finite clause into the finite one:

> She, spinning around, saw her mother . . .

Alternatively we can convert *spinning round* into a finite clause with its own subject (*she*) and finite verb (the simple past tense):

> As she spun around,
> When she spun around, } she saw her mother . . .

The second non-finite clause is *pointing the shotgun at the honeysuckle wall*. Its implicit subject *her mother* is not the subject of its own clause. A finite alternative would require an explicit subject and a progressive form of the verb:

> she saw her mother, who was pointing the shotgun at the honeysuckle wall

Non-finite clauses often imply a time relationship to their main clause. However, in this last example we have replaced the non-finite clause with a relative clause, which adds information to the noun group it's attached to.

In the original sentence there are only two finite verbs, *saw* and *glimpsed*, which are the basis of two parallel clauses joined by *and*. But there are still more processes contained in non-finite clauses — for example:

> following the direction of the gun   entwined there

Each of these can be readily expanded into finite clauses:

> when she followed the direction of the gun   which was entwined there

The point is that it's unnecessary to be as explicit as this, or to repeat *she* so often. As the original text shows, non-finite clauses allow some of the action to be expressed very economically — as long as the implied relationships between the clauses can be recognised by the reader.

Sometimes a sentence begins with a non-finite clause which is not attached to the subject of the clause immediately following, as in this example:

Being made of glass, we had to handle the table very carefully.

This use of the non-finite verb is commonly known as a 'hanging participle'. Even though the meaning is usually clear, there is a disjunction between the intended meaning and the meaning suggested by the positioning of the clauses which can lead to some quite comic interpretations. On this ground alone, it's a usage best avoided; however, a more compelling reason is that it puts a small but unnecessary roughness in the reader's path. In the example above, a finite clause like *As it was made of glass* would smooth the way.

There is another type of non-finite clause which makes use of the infinitive forms of the verb (that is, the forms that can be preceded by *to*). Here are two examples, with the non-finite clauses in italics:

He was going to come back *just to have a look* before he decided.

I hereby give my permission for my son/daughter ....
to attend the excursion.

Embedded clauses

So far we have looked at several ways in which clauses can be brought together in the one sentence to express various meanings. In the kind of sentences we've considered each clause remains a distinct entity, even if it's dependent on another clause. However, a clause can be absorbed into another clause in such a way as to become part of a component in that other clause. For instance, it might become part of a post-modifier in a noun group, in which case it is said to be **embedded** in the noun group. Below are some examples of noun groups with an embedded finite clause which were introduced in Chapter 5. In each one the clause helps to define the thing it refers to:

the house that Jack built

the table which was left to me by my aunt

the insect pests that damage crops

Non-finite clauses can be embedded in a noun group too:

the table left to me by my aunt

a paper delivered to the house

An embedded clause may look exactly like a dependent clause providing additional information, for they are both relative clauses. But though they are potentially the same in form, they are different in function, and it's important to be aware of what distinguishes them. The difference can be seen in these two examples:

> The public accounts committee is looking closely at members of parliament who misuse their travelling allowances.

> The public accounts committee is looking closely at members of parliament, who misuse their travelling allowances.

The only difference in the written forms is the comma after *parliament* in the second example. But the comma is crucial to the meaning. The first example implies that the accounts committee is looking only at certain members of parliament: namely, those who misuse their travelling allowances. The relative clause identifies which members are involved. It is an embedded clause — part of a noun group — and is traditionally known as a **restrictive** or **defining** relative clause. The second example implies that the committee is looking closely at all members of parliament; the relative clause *who misuse their travelling allowances* simply adds extra information about members of parliament in general. It is a **non-restrictive** relative clause and is dependent on the main clause, not embedded in a noun group. The meaning of the two sentences is thus quite different (indeed, it's much harder to imagine a context in which one might encounter the second in precisely this form).

A non-restrictive relative clause can be omitted without radically altering the central meaning of the sentence to which it belongs, whereas a restrictive (or embedded) relative clause cannot. In speech, a non-restrictive clause will have its own intonation pattern, often preceded by a slight pause. In writing, such clauses are usually separated from the rest of the sentence by commas, whereas an embedded clause cannot be separated in this way.

Another example, referring to macadamia trees, comes from Text 5.2:

> The two species which produce edible nuts have quite distinct characteristics.

There are actually seven species of macadamia but only two produce edible nuts. The clause *which produce edible nuts* restricts the reference of the sentence to these two species; it is an embedded clause. By contrast, the following sentence contains a relative clause which simply adds extra information:

> At the time of the attack, there were several other children and adults in the restricted area, which was clearly marked.

Which was clearly marked does not define *area*, and so it is not embedded but dependent.

It is possible, though not usual, to have both types of relative clause in the one sentence. This example refers to the 1989 sugar crop:

> The rain that has fallen this year, a lot of which came from the cyclone, should give us a bumper crop.

The clause *that has fallen this year* is embedded; it defines which rain is being referred to. However, *a lot of which came from the cyclone* is not embedded; it is simply an additional piece of information about the rain and is a dependent clause, hierarchically related to the main clause.

Although restrictive and non-restrictive relative clauses are formally almost exactly the same, there is one significant difference affecting the pronouns which introduce them. Besides *who, whom, which* and *whose*, it is also possible — indeed quite common — to use *that* as a relative pronoun in restrictive clauses. It can be used instead any of the others except *whose* — for example:

> Many of the Cambodians are young men that have left because . . .
>
> the Cambodians that the Indonesians are holding on Galang
>
> the rain that has fallen this year
>
> the house that Jack built

Quite frequently *that* can be omitted, as long as it's not the subject of its clause:

> the Cambodians the Indonesians are holding on Galang
>
> the house Jack built

Summary and links with traditional grammar

A clause can be an independent sentence. On the other hand, several clauses can be brought together to form one sentence. These can be linked as clauses of equal status (parallel clauses) or bound together in a hierarchy with one clause dependent on another. Both of these general types of relationship can be used for introducing additional information, for referring to time and for logical relationships. There are also embedded clauses, which are part of a noun group. Both dependent and embedded clauses can be either finite or non-finite.

In traditional grammar, parallel clauses are referred to as *co-ordinate* clauses, while clauses related in a hierarchy are referred to as *main* and *subordinate*. Several different types of subordinate clause are recognised, and they are broadly similar to some of the relationships discussed in this chapter. The general distinction between dependent and embedded is not made in traditional grammar, though the more specific distinction between non-restrictive and restrictive relative clauses is recognised. One traditional type which has not yet been discussed is the noun clause; in functional grammar this is treated as a form of *projection*, which is the subject of the next chapter.

Projecting
the Message

In the last chapter we explored how several clauses can be brought together in the one sentence to express messages more complex than those that can be conveyed in a single clause. However, a simple message can also be developed in another way, known as **projection**. It's rather like the idea of taking on a role and projecting the voice, as stage actors do. For, often in writing and sometimes in speech, we take what someone else has said and 'say' it ourselves, making it part of our own message. Thus we project it. It's essentially a simple and familiar concept, but it can be adapted to many purposes.

Quoted words

TEXT 10.1 FROM A CONVERSATION BETWEEN TWO PASSENGERS ON AN AIRCRAFT

'How come you're on this charter anyway?' said the girl.
'One of my students sold me her ticket,' he replied.
'Now all is clear,' said the girl. 'I figured you couldn't be needing an abortion.'

(adapted from David Lodge, *Changing Places*)

In the world created by this fictional text, some words are spoken: a woman asks a question, a man replies and the woman then comments. The spoken words are written within inverted commas and the speakers are identified outside them. These simple means allow us to project any piece of language: a word, a phrase, a clause, a sentence, several sentences — even a whole speech! But, to explore how projection works, we'll take the clause as a typical case.

Let's start with the man's reply in Text 10.1: *'One of my students sold me her ticket'*. That clause is attached to another which identifies the speaker: *he replied*. The relationship between the two clauses is shown mainly by the punctuation and the fact that they are placed side by side. The speaker's words are said to be *projected* by the clause which follows them. So:

'One of my students sold me her ticket,'	he replied.
projected clause *(the speaker's actual words)*	projecting clause *(identifying speaker and verbal process)*

There are many variations on this pattern. The projecting clause may come before the speaker's words instead of after, or it may be placed in between two parts of what the speaker is saying, as where the girl comments on the man's reply. Sometimes subject and process will be inverted in the projecting clause, as in:

'How come you're on this charter anyway?' said the girl.

And often, if it's clear who the speaker is, there will be no projecting clause but just the speaker's words enclosed in inverted commas.

The projecting clause can serve not only to identify the speaker but also to indicate how the words were said — rather like stage directions. This can be done either by lexical variation (i.e. by using a different process) or syntactically, by means of an adverbial expression:

'You're leading!' he yelled.

'Oh, we're new here,' Kath answered politely.

All these instances of projection where the speaker's actual words are quoted are referred to as **direct speech**.

Reported words

Another very common type of projection involves a different way of representing the speaker's words. Let's try adapting Text 10.1:

The girl asked how he came to be on that charter.
He replied that one of his students had sold him her ticket.
The girl said that now all was clear; she figured he couldn't have been needing an abortion.

This version doesn't claim that the actual words of the speakers are quoted. What's given is the meaning of what they said — the ideas, not all the actual words. This is an example of what is referred to as **indirect speech** or **reported speech**. What's involved can be summarised like this:

1 The projecting clause, based on a verbal process and identifying the speaker, is more or less essential and usually comes first, as in our example:

The girl asked   He replied   The girl said

2 The projected clause, representing what the speaker said, often begins with *that*, though it's sometimes omitted (e.g. *He said he was a lecturer*). However, if the speaker asked a question, some interrogative word is used instead. (Indirect questions will be discussed more fully below.)

The two ways of presenting speech, direct and indirect, can be aligned with the two different ways of relating clauses which were explained in the previous chapter. The projecting and projected clauses of direct speech are of equal status and can be regarded as parallel clauses. On the other hand, the projected clause of indirect speech is dependent on its projecting clause and so these clauses are arranged in a hierarchy.

Any text may contain a mixture of direct speech and indirect speech. Many narratives are enlivened by the immediacy of dialogue in direct speech, and yet there are occasions where the indirect reporting of speech is just as effective. Some writers strive for a balance between the two modes. And sometimes, especially in newspaper reports, the distinction between them is blurred by minimal punctuation.

The distancing of reported speech

There are some systematic relationships between the words given in indirect speech and the actual words the speaker is supposed to have said. Compare these extracts:

> 'Now all is clear,' said the girl. 'I figured you couldn't be needing an abortion.'

> The girl said that now all was clear; she figured he couldn't have been needing an abortion.

The speech role pronouns of the actual words (*I* and *you*) are replaced by reference pronouns (*she* and *he*) in indirect speech. There is also a change in the time frame: *is* becomes *was*, *couldn't be needing* becomes *couldn't have been needing*. This is also evident in the preceding part of the text:

> 'One of my students sold me her ticket,' he replied.

> He replied that one of his students had sold him her ticket.

The effect of these changes is to distance the report from the original context in which the words were spoken. Since the speech is reported at a later time, some distancing is inevitable, and it occurs both in factual recounts and in narrative fiction. It begins with the projecting clause, where the verb is generally past tense. The effect of this is carried through to the projected clause, where the original verb is often shifted into the past (or further into the past) and speech role pronouns become reference pronouns. There can also be distancing of place as well as time; a demonstrative *this* becomes *that*.

Thus we have in English a set of resources by which we can record a conversation, or parts of a conversation. We can do so either directly (where the speakers' actual words are included) or indirectly (where those words are transposed into a different key). These speech-recording resources are used mainly in written English (for example, in novels, short stories, biography and newspaper reports), but they are also used in speech to recount some earlier conversation.

Questions and commands

So far we have concentrated on what happens to statements (declarative structures) in projected clauses. Now we need to examine more systematically what happens to questions and commands (interrogative and imperative structures). They are referred to as **indirect questions** and **indirect commands**.

Projected *yes/no* questions are introduced by the conjunctions *if* or *whether*:

> 'Is this the way to the Entertainment Centre?' she asked.

> She asked if/whether that was the way to the Entertainment Centre.

Alternative questions also make use of *if* or *whether*:

> 'Would you like tea or coffee?' he asked.

> He asked if/whether she would like tea or coffee.

WH questions make use of their own WH word:

> 'What time does the show start?' she asked.

> She asked what time the show started.

The distancing of speech role, place and time applies to all these interrogatives, just as it does to declaratives. Another systematic difference between the original questions and their projected versions is that the normal inversions of direct speech do not apply. In the projected clause the subject precedes the finite element (e.g. first auxiliary), and if a dummy first auxiliary has been brought in to form the original question (e.g. *does* in the last example), it disappears.

Projected commands involve greater changes. Essentially they make use of a non-finite clause.

> He said: 'Tidy up your room!'   He told me to tidy up my room.

There is also a change in the verbal process; the original *said* becomes *told* and the participant receiving the command (the beneficiary *me*) is made explicit. This means that a speech role pronoun comes into the projecting clause, and that in turn affects the speech role of the pronoun in the projected clause. However, there are other possibilities depending on the original context — for example:

> He said: 'Tidy up your room!'   { He told her to tidy up her room.
>   { He told him to tidy up his room.

In the last example *his room* is ambiguous as it stands, but it probably wouldn't be in context.

Reported thoughts

The model of indirect speech makes some further developments possible. Consider these examples:

> He believes that the world is flat.
>
> We know that the world is not flat.
>
> I feel that everyone is turning against me.
>
> We thought there would be someone here to meet us.
>
> I fear we're going to run out of money.
>
> I wonder what became of her.

In each of these sentences there are essentially two clauses, the second one being projected from the first. But the projected clauses don't represent speech so much as thoughts, feelings or beliefs. All these things could have been said, of course, but they're not presented that way in these examples. They are presented as ideas rather than as snippets of conversation. And they are projected from mental processes rather than verbal processes. We might call them 'indirect thoughts' except that the term doesn't seem as appropriate as 'indirect speech', for unless we're blessed with ESP, we can't perceive thoughts directly. In fact, even though it's possible to present thoughts 'directly' (as in *'What became of her?' I wondered*), the indirect version is the normal one.

In other respects reported thoughts are similar to indirect speech. Most of them begin with *that* — at least potentially. However, *that* is not essential and it has been omitted from two of the examples above. Note too that the last example, being a WH question, begins with the interrogative *what* in both its direct and indirect versions.

Double projection

Let's return to the last remark in Text 10.1:

> . . . said the girl. 'I figured you couldn't be needing an abortion.'

This of course is an example of direct speech. But if we look at the actual words quoted, we find two clauses, the second of which (*you couldn't be needing an abortion*) is projected from the first (*I figured*). The projected clause is an idea 'figured' in the mind of the girl.

What we have here is a double projection. It becomes more obvious in an indirect version, where the middle clause is both projected and projecting:

The girl said   that she figured   he couldn't have been needing an abortion.

	projecting	projected
projecting	projected	

Now let's look at a more complex example of double projection from a news report about a candidate in a US presidential campaign:

> The Miami Herald claimed Mr Hart was lying when he said reporters had refused to interview Miami model Miss Donna Rice, 29, and another young woman last Friday night, was lying when he said the paper conceded it might have got the story wrong, and was lying when he said that he had approached the reporters, not the other way around.

The basic projecting clause is *The Miami Herald claimed*. The first projected clause is *Mr Hart was lying* and it's immediately followed by a time clause, *when he said*, which is also a projecting clause. These parts of the text can be represented thus:

The Miami Herald claimed	Mr Hart was lying	when he said
		time/projecting
projecting	projected	

The pattern established in *Mr Hart was lying when he said* is repeated twice and so serves to introduce each of the three alleged lies — namely:

> reporters had refused . . .
>
> the paper conceded . . .
>
> that he had approached the reporters . . .

The second instance (*the paper conceded*) also functions as a projecting clause, bringing in a third level of projection with the clause *it might have got the story wrong*. Even the first one (*reporters had refused*) is a projecting clause with a non-finite projection, though what was said is implied rather than stated. Note that in all the finite projected clauses (and there are seven including repetitions) the word *that* is used only once, though it could have been used for every one.

Here is an analysis which shows all the clause relationships:

A	The Miami Herald claimed	*projecting*
B1	Mr Hart was lying	*projected*
C	when he said	*time/projecting*
D	reporters had refused	*projected/projecting*
E	to interview Miami model Miss Donna Rice, 29, and another young woman last Friday night,	*projected* *(non-finite)*
B2	was lying	*projected*
C	when he said	*time/projecting*
D	the paper conceded	*projected/projecting*
E	it might have got the story wrong	*projected*

B3	and was lying	*projected*
C	when he said	*time/projecting*
D	that he had approached the reporters, not the other way around.	*projected*

Embedded projections

There is a group of nouns which refer to things that can be said or thought. Some of them are nominalised processes, such as *claim, assertion, admission, announcement, belief* and so on. Others are words which refer to messages of one kind or another. The word *message* itself is one; other examples are *news, fact, idea* and *illusion*. Any of these nouns can be qualified by a projected clause conveying the idea referred to by the noun, in which case the projected clause is embedded in a noun group. Here are some examples:

> The news that there had been an earthquake in Newcastle caught us by surprise.
> (*cf.* The news of the Newcastle earthquake caught us by surprise.)
> I had an idea that someone was going to meet me.
> The fact that light travels at a finite but very high speed was first discovered in 1676 by the Danish astronomer Ole Christensen Roemer.

Sometimes a verb appears to be projecting a clause when it is actually being projected from one of these nouns, though the noun has been omitted. Compare these two examples:

> I regret that the old theatre has been pulled down.
> I regret the fact that the old theatre has been pulled down.

Sometimes a projected clause qualifying one of these nouns resembles a relative clause performing a similar role, though the effect is quite different:

> We received a message that the ship's engines had failed.
> We received a message that threw us into a panic.

It is possible for projected clauses to appear be independent of any projecting element (either verb or noun), as in this example:

> That we had to get out of the building was obvious.

Here the projected clause is the subject of the sentence, but in sentences like these it's more usual to have a dummy subject, so that the projected clause is at the end:

> It was obvious that we had to get out of the building.

In any case the projected clause is embedded because potentially the sentence has this form:

> The fact that we had to get out of the building was obvious.

Summary

The main types of projection are summarised in the following table (based on Halliday 1985, pp. 231, 233):

	Speech	Thought
Direct *(actual words)* statement	He said: 'They have lost the keys.'	He thought: 'They have lost the keys.'
question	He asked: 'Have they lost the keys?'	He wondered: 'Have they lost the keys?'
command	He warned: 'Don't lose the keys.'	
Indirect *(meaning)* statement	He said that they had lost the keys.	He thought that they had lost the keys.
question	He asked if they had lost the keys.	He wondered if they had lost the keys.
command	He warned them not to lose the keys.	
Embedded	The accusation that they had lost the keys . . . The belief that they had lost the keys . . . The fact that they had lost the keys . . . That they had lost the keys . . . The question of whether they had lost the keys . . . The warning not to lose the keys . . .	

The
Developing Text

In Chapter 1 we introduced three major functions of language, namely:

- acting upon the world (the *interpersonal* function)
- reflecting the world and making sense of it (the *experiential* function)
- making connections within the text and to the context (the *textual* function).

We have now explored some of the grammatical implications of the first two and it's time to deal with the third, the textual function.

Most of the grammar we've been considering so far has taken the clause as the basic unit for expressing a message, and so we have looked at the clause itself, at elements of structure within the clause and at connections between clauses in a sentence. Yet when we use language our texts usually continue over more than one sentence, and many important grammatical relationships and structures can only be appreciated fully when we look at how they fit into a text extending over several sentences.

It is just these relationships and structures which help to give texts an overall coherence, so that we recognise them as texts rather than random collections of sentences. And it is this aspect of grammar which fulfils the textual function of language, enabling us to make connections both within the text and between the text and its context.

In constructing any text, the speaker or writer will have certain things to say and will often want to have a certain effect on the audience. He or she will also make assumptions about what information can be taken for granted and what the listener or reader will be able to guess. All this will affect the way in which the ideas are expressed and the order in which they are presented. Moreover, as the text unfolds and further meanings are made explicit, the assumptions will be constantly reassessed. For the accumulation of meaning in the text affects the way each successive part is expressed and how it is related to what has gone before.

In this chapter we'll consider two ways of organising meaning in a text. One is the way in which the speaker/writer can present information as either *given* or *new* for the listener/reader. The other is the way in which the speaker/writer chooses something as the starting point or *theme* of each clause in the text, and how the succession of these themes contributes to the development of meaning over the whole text. We'll first deal with each of these notions as they operate within the clause; then we'll consider how they help to develop a longer text. But first we'll need a sample text.

TEXT 11.1 PART OF A TV COMMENTARY ON THE START OF A YACHT RACE

The commentary team consists of Jane, a general news broadcaster; Ken, a professional yachting commentator, and David, a well-known yachtsman.

JANE: How many sails would these leading maxis carry, Ken? 'Sovereign' for example.

KEN: 'Sovereign' for example would have twenty plus bags of sails on board and most of them are made of all these latest exotic materials like kevlar, and they're stronger than steel now, the sails. David, having been involved in the South Australian America's Cup campaign, could certainly tell us a lot about how sail cloths have changed and how much better they are, these er . . . the brown kevlar sails and things like that, Dave.

DAVID: Yes, it's amazing, and now of course they pull the boats to pieces. That's the trouble. In the old days the old skippers used to say, 'Leave it up there. If there's too much sail up it'll blow off.' But nowadays the mast comes down with it.

JANE: And that's a big mast to come down. Look at it. That's the biggest maxi now in the world going round; that's certainly the biggest mast.

KEN: Well over 30 metres of aluminium extrusion there and er . . . that's a huge sail plan. The spinnaker there on that boat, that's made of a dacron-type material and the mainsail has er . . . the back edge is usually dacron or mylar, kevlar and er . . . very, very strong materials they're using in these sails now certainly, as David said; the sails don't blow off any more — the quickest way to reef a boat now is to be dismasted.

This transcript is of course deficient in two respects: the punctuation is only a rough guide to the intonation patterns of the speakers, and there is no equivalent for the succession of visual images that was an integral part of the original broadcast.

So what's new?

As we have indicated, in every clause of a text the speaker or writer can present the meanings to the listener or reader either as information that is **given** or as something **new**. The choice will be based on the speaker's assumptions about what can be taken for granted at any point in the text, including what the listener is likely to recover from what has already been said. (I say speaker and listener here merely for convenience, for the same applies to writers and readers.) This continual exercise of choice has a number of important grammatical consequences.

In any clause there is a tendency to work from the known to the unknown, from the Given to the New (from now on we'll use capitals to show when Given and New are being used as technical terms). So the speaker usually begins with what he or she assumes the listener will already know — as if to say, 'Here's what you already know and now here's something new.'

Let's see what happens at the beginning of Text 11.1:

JANE: How many sails would these leading maxis carry, Ken? 'Sovereign' for example.

KEN: 'Sovereign' for example would have twenty plus bags of sails on board . . .

Taking Jane's question first, we must accept that the topic of 'sails' has already been introduced into the commentary and that the leading maxis are in view, and so these elements can be taken as Given. What is New is *How many* and *carry*. The different elements can be shown like this:

How many	sails	would	these leading maxis	carry?
New	Given	New	Given	New

One key word of the New elements, *carry*, comes at the end of the clause. This is the basic tendency in English — that is, New elements tend to come at the end of the clause, preceded by the Given. However, many variations on this pattern commonly occur, and this question beginning with *How many*, another New element, is just one of them.

The arrangement of Given and New elements in the clause is more obvious in speech than in writing, because in speech it is supported by the intonation pattern (indeed, it can be established by the intonation pattern). How we say the clause helps to establish the meaning of what we are saying.

This tie-up between intonation and meaning gives the speaker more immediate flexibility than the writer in the arrangement of Given and New information (the writer, denied intonation, must rely on other devices, some of which will be discussed later in the chapter). Essentially what happens in speech is that the major stress in the clause is placed on the key element of the New information. This can be illustrated from the opening of Ken's response:

'Sovereign' for example would have twenty plus bags of sails on board . . .

The New element is *twenty plus*. The major stress falls on *plus*, with an almost equally strong stress on *twen-*. Everything that precedes the New is Given (in fact, it is almost word-for-word repetition). What follows *plus* is also Given (including *bags of sails*, which Ken treats as equivalent to *sails*), and that points to something significant. To give the answer sooner, the New has been brought nearer the beginning of the clause — an arrangement marked by the intonation pattern, where the level of stress tails off towards the end.

There's another kind of flexibility more readily available to the speaker. We have suggested that the intonation pattern applies to the clause, and indeed this is the typical arrangement. However, it too can be varied, for essentially the intonation pattern defines its own domain — it sets its own boundaries. That domain is called the **tone group**.

A clause can be divided into several tone groups, which are generally separated by pauses. Each group has its own main stress, which is referred to as the **tonic** element, and thus its own bit of New information specially highlighted. Here are two examples from Text 11.1, with the tonic syllables underlined and the tone group boundaries marked //:

> //and most of them are made of all these latest exotic ma<u>te</u>rials//like <u>kev</u>lar//

> //In the <u>old</u> days//the <u>old</u> skippers used to say//

A clause is often broken up into several separate tone groups when the speaker is placing emphasis on each segment. In a written text the same effect can be achieved by the use of commas — as in this next example, which derives from the published version of a paper originally delivered orally:

> When I was seven there were no plastics, there were no organ transplants, no computers, no jets, no satellites, no lasers, no transistors, no oral contraceptives . . .

The writer/speaker wants each of these technical developments to be stressed; each one is a new piece of information in the text. The commas mark off what in speech would be a succession of separate tone groups. (This is in fact one of the conventional uses of the comma: to separate items in a list that forms part of a longer text.)

Clearly the treatment of parts of a clause as Given and parts as New is mainly influenced by what precedes the clause, but it may also affect the way that succeeding information is presented — how the next clause will begin and so on. And that leads us to the question of theme.

Jumping-off points

Speakers and writers have choices when they start clauses, but the choices aren't random. What the speaker or writer chooses as the first element in the clause is distinctly important in English; it represents a kind of jumping-off point, as if the speaker or writer were saying, 'Here's what I'm on about in this clause.' Referred to as the **theme**, it includes everything in the clause up to and including the first participant, circumstance or process. The remainder of the clause, where the theme can be developed, is referred to as the **rheme**.

The choice of theme in a clause will be strongly influenced by what has preceded it (unless it is the first clause in the text) and by what the speaker or writer plans to follow it with. But there is no simple rule, and choice always rests with the speaker or writer. Let's see how it works by considering part of Ken's first response to Jane in terms of theme and rheme:

'Sovereign' for example	would have twenty plus bags of sails . . .
theme	rheme

and most of them	are made of all these latest exotic materials . . .
theme	rheme

and they	're stronger than steel now, the sails.
theme	rheme

Ken picks up Jane's suggestion that he use 'Sovereign' as an example and so his first theme, *'Sovereign' for example*, precisely echoes her request. Then, since he wants to make two more points about the sails, the next two clauses have themes which refer to them. He also wants to mark the continuity and so these themes begin with the linking word *and*.

The presence of *and* in these last two themes suggests that the theme is potentially more than a jumping-off point for the rheme. In fact it can include elements related to all three of the major language functions resumed at the beginning of this chapter. In the examples above, *'Sovereign' for example, most of them* and *they* are all **topical** elements — that is, they relate to the topic of the clause and, more broadly, to the experiential function of language. The topical element is essential in any theme. The two *ands* are **textual** elements and relate to the textual function of language. Since their job is to make connections across the boundaries of clauses, textual elements (which are optional) are most commonly placed on the boundary, right at the beginning of the clause.

These two elements are the most important in the structure of the theme; essentially textual elements look back to the preceding text, while topical elements point forward to the development of the clause in the rheme. The third possible element, the **interpersonal**, is somewhat less common. It may take the form of a vocative, as in:

> *Sandra*, your shoe's undone

or a word indicating the speaker's attitude:

> *Surely* you had it yesterday.

It's quite possible to combine all three elements in the one theme:

> *But unfortunately she* had to decline.

Textual, interpersonal, topical is the normal order of elements, as in the last example.

The themes discussed so far are typical of those found in independent clauses. However, when a dependent clause is placed first in the sentence, it functions as the theme. Consider this mirror pair of examples:

> I'll be ready when you arrive.
>
> When you arrive I'll be ready.

In the first the theme is the topical element *I*; in the second it's the whole clause *when you arrive*. The effect is a slight shift of focus from the activity of the 'I' to the activity of the 'you'. Dependent clauses introduced by *if, although, before, since* and so on can equally occupy the thematic position in a sentence while retaining their own internal thematic structure.

Marked and unmarked themes

In a declarative clause the subject is normally the theme, and since this is the normal pattern, it's called an **unmarked** theme:

> 'Sovereign' for example would have twenty plus . . .

If something else is chosen as theme, it tends to stand out; this is called a **marked** theme. In the example below the marked theme is italicised; the subject of the clause has become part of the rheme:

> *In the old days* the old skippers used to say

As might be expected, interrogative clauses behave a little differently. In a WH question the unmarked theme will be the interrogative word or group — for example, *How many sails* in:

> How many sails would these leading maxis carry, Ken?

In a *yes/no* question the finite element (first auxiliary) and subject constitute the unmarked theme — for example, *Did you* in:

> Did you remember to turn off the gas?

So the grammar of the interrogative is tied in with the theme position. The same applies to imperatives, where it is the process which is the unmarked theme — for example, *leave* in:

> Leave it up there.

Nevertheless both interrogatives and imperatives can have marked themes when a circumstance precedes the interrogative word(s) or the verb — as in:

> *In six months' time* what do you think the position will be?
>
> *Carefully* cut along the dotted line.

The marked theme is a useful device because it enables us to take a component out of the rheme and give it the prominence and emphasis of the thematic position. When teachers advise children to find 'good sentence openings', the examples they give are often marked themes. But while it's true that they can help to avoid monotony of style, too many of them will defeat the purpose.

Thematic variation

We'll now look at a passage showing how a variation in the pattern of themes can be used to mark a significant point in the story:

> I shall never forget a car ride I once took with Atyeo in New York. He was leaving to return to Paris by ship. We left the hotel late and became caught in rush-hour traffic. We heard police sirens behind us and there swept past a cavalcade of large black limousines. Atyeo exclaimed, 'It's Vyshinsky' (the Soviet Minister of Justice of the time) and ordered our driver to join the back of the cavalcade. We raced to the docks with the Russian security guards in the car ahead watching every move. No one could ever accuse Atyeo of a lack of resourcefulness.
>
> (Alan Renouf, *The Champagne Trail*)

Most of the clauses begin with references to people who are the agents: *I, he, we, Atyeo* and *no one*. These are unmarked themes and all but the last consist of given information. But notice what happens in the fourth sentence:

> We heard police sirens behind us and there swept past a cavalcade of large black limousines.

In the second of the two parallel clauses the theme is *and there swept,* and the agent, *a cavalcade of large black limousines*, is moved to the end, where it is more prominent. Compare this with the more conventional order of components in a declarative clause, with the agent in theme position:

> a cavalcade of large black limousines swept past

The order that the writer has chosen gets the most significant part of the New information into the position of end-focus, where in speech it would receive tonic stress. The slight delay in its delivery is a dramatic touch.

Bringing things into focus

We can say that the two positions in the clause offering the greatest potential for emphasis are the beginning (the theme position) and the end (which tends to feature New information). There are several devices in English for changing the order of components in the clause in order to bring things into focus in either position. Some examples have already been noted; others include this one from Text 11.1:

> very very strong materials they're using in these sails now certainly

Here the effect is placed in theme position ahead of the agent. Yet this is simply a change of order. A grammatically more complex change is the active/passive variation, which could be applied thus:

> very very strong materials are being used in these sails now certainly

But because the effect is now the subject of the clause (as is normal with the passive), the theme becomes unmarked and the emphasis is slightly less.

In each of the following examples a different component is chosen as the theme:

> Pigeon House Mountain was named by Captain Cook.   *(passive)*
>
> Captain Cook named Pigeon House Mountain.   *(active)*

If the discourse were about Pigeon House Mountain, the passive version is the more likely one. Indeed, taken out of context, the active clause seems to imply that this was all Cook did. However, another grammatical device, an identifying clause, allows us to have Captain Cook in thematic position without minimising his other achievements:

> It was Captain Cook who named Pigeon House Mountain.

The next group of examples (adapted from Text 11.2) illustrates the same grammatical possibilities, together with one further device:

> Plant and animal fossils provide evidence for the existence of Gondwana.
>
> Evidence for the existence of Gondwana is provided by plant and animal fossils.
>
> It is plant and animal fossils that provide evidence for the existence of Gondwana.
>
> What provides evidence for the existence of Gondwana is plant and animal fossils.

In the last example the theme is identified by means of a WH clause. However, the main point is that all these grammatical devices (and many others) allow us to order our clauses and sentences so as bring the appropriate components into focus as themes or as New information in end position. This is usually done in terms of the way the clause fits into the text being composed, with an eye to strengthening its overall cohesion. In other words, what is best as theme and what New information is to be presented in end position is not determined on the basis of the clause alone but in terms of the whole text — and ultimately the context as well.

Developing the text

So far in this chapter we've concentrated on ways of organising meaning within the clause, especially the arrangement of Given and New information and the selection of one component of the clause as its theme. We'll now explore further how these arrangements within clauses affect the development of meaning through whole texts. We'll use two examples, one spoken and one written.

David's comments and the first part of Jane's reply from Text 11.1 provide us with one example. They are set out below with the themes in boxes and the tonic syllables, stressing New information, underlined:

$\boxed{\text{Yes, it}}$'s amazing

$\boxed{\text{and now}}$ of course they pull the <u>boats</u> to pieces

$\boxed{\text{That}}$'s the <u>troub</u>le

$\boxed{\text{In the <u>old</u> days}}$ the <u>old</u> skippers used to say

$\boxed{\text{Leave}}$ it <u>up</u> there

$\boxed{\text{If there's too much sail up}}$ it'll <u>blow</u> off

$\boxed{\text{But <u>nowadays</u>}}$ the mast comes down <u>with</u> it

$\boxed{\text{And that}}$'s a <u>big</u> mast to come down

We can see three kinds of theme here. The most obvious are the marked themes referring to time:

<blockquote>and now   in the old days   but nowadays</blockquote>

The contrast between sails now and sails as they used to be has already been implied by Ken, and these time themes serve to highlight the contrast. Interspersed with them are unmarked themes which refer back to things previously mentioned:

<blockquote>Yes, it   That   And that</blockquote>

Finally there are the themes in the words attributed to the old skippers:

<blockquote>Leave   *(a process theme marking the imperative structure)*

If there's too much sail up   *(a clause theme introducing a condition)*</blockquote>

If we now look at these themes in sequence, the development will be clearer. (The quotation from the old skippers is a kind of embedded section within the main text.)

<blockquote>

Yes, it   *(agreement, backward reference)*

and now   *(continuity, time)*

That   *(backward reference)*

In the old days   *(time)*

Leave   *(process)*

If there's too much sail up   *(condition)*

But nowadays   *(contrast, time)*

And that   *(continuity, backward reference)*

</blockquote>

Much of what David says is New. The focus of this New information — the tonic stress — tends to come towards the end of the clauses except where there are marked themes, which are tone groups in their own right. For instance, when David wants to emphasise the old/new contrast with some reminiscence, he signals his change of direction with *in the old days*, a marked theme of New material which is a separate tone group with its own tonic stress.

For our second example we turn to the written text we drew on in the last section. The major themes are again shown in boxes, but of course there are no stress marks.

TEXT 11.2 AN EXTRACT FROM A TEXTBOOK

The study of fossils and rock layers also adds to our knowledge of the earth's history. Geologists have uncovered plant and animal fossils which show that 225 million years ago the continents were all joined together as one great landmass. Over millions of years this supercontinent, which we call Pangaea, gradually split up into a northern landmass called Laurasia and a southern one called Gondwana. Eventually Gondwana also drifted apart into the continents we know today.

Fossil plants and animals discovered in Antarctica have been found on the other continents that once formed the southern landmass. They provide very strong evidence for the existence of Gondwana, because the plants and animals could not have spread if the continents were separated by oceans.

(C. Heath, *Australians in Antarctica*)

We can see that the first two themes are concerned with the study of natural phenomena and only indirectly with the phenomena themselves. The next theme is in a clause which is projected from an embedded clause; yet this projection is the device for introducing the main thesis of the text — that is, the theoretical position reached through the study mentioned at the beginning. The themes of the projected clause and the next two clauses highlight a major element in that theory: namely, time and the passage of time. The second part of the text, which is a separate paragraph, presents an argument in support of the thesis. The themes in this paragraph involve the natural phenomena and logical relationships that constitute the argument.

The thematic development of the text can be summarised as follows:

The study of fossils and rock layers	*(scientific research)*
Geologists	*(agents of the research)*
that 225 million years ago	*(time reference)*
Over millions of years	*(passage of time)*
Eventually	*(passage of time)*
Fossil plants and animals discovered in Antarctica	*(phenomena)*

They	(backward reference to the phenomena)
because the plants and animals	(logical argument involving the
if the continents	phenomena)

A great deal of this text is New, especially in the first part where the thesis is being introduced, stated and elaborated. Once that groundwork is established, each clause contains some Given information, which generally comes earlier in the clause, leaving the position of end-focus free for New information. In some clauses, however, the distinction between Given and New is not clear-cut; there is a gradation from one to the other.

Links with traditional grammar

In this chapter we have touched on some aspects of traditional grammar, such as the active/passive option, and some aspects of traditional teaching, such as 'good sentence openings'. All of them are best understood in terms of the ordering of components within clauses so that they best fit the overall text. The more comprehensive functional view of this takes into account aspects of the language system — the deployment of Given and New information and the choice of clause theme — which were not recognised in traditional grammar. Yet, because of their importance for the development of a text, they are both vital resources for language users.

The Cohesive Text

The author of a text, whether spoken or written, normally assumes that as it unfolds the listener or reader will absorb more and more of what it's about and so will be able to recover an increasing amount of what has gone before. This assumption encourages the author to make use of certain grammatical devices which show that the various parts of the text are related to each other — an interrelatedness known as **cohesion**.

The devices which help to bind the text together and establish its unity are known as **cohesive devices**. The main ones are *reference, ellipsis and substitution, lexical cohesion* and *conjunction,* and we will now look at each of them in turn.

Reference

Once something has been introduced into a text, it can be referred to again and again (if necessary) by means of short words which save us having to repeat the original longer word or group. A simple example occurs in these two sentences from Text 11.2:

> Fossil plants and animals discovered in Antarctica have been found on other continents that once formed the southern landmass. They provide very strong evidence for the existence of Gondwana.

The theme of the first sentence, *fossil plants and animals discovered in Antarctica,* is represented in the next sentence by the single word *they.*

Pronouns

As the example above shows, something originally represented by a noun group can be referred to again by means of the reference pronouns. The basic reference pronouns are *he, she, it* and *they,* and they are set out with their related forms on p. 66. Each has a general meaning: that is, either singular or plural, and, if singular, either male, female or inanimate. However, they derive their precise meaning from whatever they refer to — which is often something already introduced into the text. In other words, the listener or reader can usually recover the full meaning or reference from the preceding text; it is part of the Given information. The following text, which forms the opening paragraph of a novel, includes a number of examples:

> After their quarrels Cullen often hid the knives. Before making up a bed in *his* study *he* would grab up the carving knife, the bread knife, and, after a particularly savage row, the assortment of sharp cleavers and fruit knives as well, and secrete *them* in the freezer or under a pile of laundry in the washtub next to the housemaids' room.
>
> (Robert Drewe, *A Cry in the Jungle Bar*)

The pronouns in italics each refer back to something already introduced into the text and their reference is clear. This type of **backward** reference is the commonest use of the reference pronouns, especially in written texts. But there are other possibilities. For instance, in the first sentence of the text above — the first sentence of the novel — there is a reference pronoun which clearly does not refer to something already in the text. 'Who are "they" who have these quarrels?' we are left wondering. We know that *their* refers to some people — probably two people, one of whom is likely to be Cullen himself — but for the rest we must read on. This is an example of **forward** reference, and its purpose here is obvious enough.

Forward reference can also occur within the one sentence, though such sentences often read rather awkwardly:

> The media at Parliament House were told by his representative that the Prime Minister would be making a statement at 4 pm.

> What happens if the classroom communicates their place in the learning hierarchy to students?

Even the more usual backward reference can sometimes lead to ambiguity, as in this fragment from a radio commentary:

> I'm carefully avoiding the piles of horse manure. I've just passed four of them, actually, attached to a yellow coach.

There had been no previous mention of horses in the commentary, and so the listener had to wait for the arrival of the yellow coach to have a chance of realising that *them* referred not to *the piles of horse manure* but to *horses*, which had been referred to only indirectly through the classifier *horse* (nouns used as classifiers are usually singular).

Reference pronouns can also be used to refer to things outside the text — usually something obvious in the situational context. This function is called **outward** reference. Unlike forward and backward reference, which refer to things in the text, outward reference is not a cohesive device, though it is a useful way of 'pointing' to things in the context. It is more likely to be found in speech than in writing, as in this example of one child speaking to another:

> You've got it all over me!

Here *it* referred to glue, which was quite obvious in the context.

Written examples are most likely to be found in public notices, such as:

> CAUTION
> Freshwater crocodiles inhabit this area.
> For your own safety
> do not approach or feed these animals.

Here the word *this* is an outward reference, pointing to the area in which the notice is situated. The other demonstrative, *these*, is a backward reference, since the animals in question have already been introduced into the text.

In bureaucratic writing there is a tendency to use *same* as a reference pronoun:

> If your department has any surplus copies of the report, please return same to this office ASAP.

This non-standard use of *same* refers to something inanimate, either singular or plural, and it is restricted to the object position. Its standard equivalents are *it* and *them*.

To sum up, there are three kinds of reference we can make by means of reference pronouns:

backward: referring to someone or something already mentioned, e.g:

> Once Mr Dewsbury had finished his breakfast he threw his manuscript on the fire and burnt it — he had never done anything on an empty stomach.

forward: referring to someone or something about to be mentioned, e.g. the two pronouns in italics below:

> Once *he* had finished *his* breakfast, Mr Dewsbury threw his manuscript on the fire and burnt it.

outward: referring to someone or something in the situation in which the language is being used — someone or something likely to be obvious to the listener (or reader).

Demonstratives

While the reference pronouns play a major part in establishing cohesion in a text, there are other resources available too. The demonstratives *this* and *that* (and their plural forms *these* and *those*) often demonstrate connections within a text. They can be used as pointers within a noun group or as pronouns (where they constitute the noun group). They assure the reader of the identity of two references — the one marked by *this* or *that* picking up one that has already occurred in the text. Here are two examples, with the demonstratives shown in italics:

> Refundable interest offer on appliance purchases:
>
> *This* offer, effective from 1st August, is available to approved credit customers.
>
> An interest rate of 18% per annum, monthly reducible, will be charged. *This* will be fully refunded following the final payment by the agreed date and provided payments have been made on time.

The demonstratives *here* and *there* can also be used to make cohesive links within a text.

Comparison

Another device for establishing cohesion is comparison. Links between items in a text can be made on the basis of their being the same, similar or different. This quiz question is an example of forward reference involving comparison:

> In the movie of the same name, what do the initials ET stand for?

Comparative reference can also be achieved with words like *other*, *more*, *less* and *fewer* and through adjectival comparison — in short, through all the grammatical resources for comparison discussed in Chapter 7.

Reference can sometimes be indicated by means of internal comparatives: i.e. *the former* and *the latter*. These are similar in function to the demonstratives, but they enable us to refer back to items already mentioned on the basis of their order in the text itself.

Ellipsis and substitution

As a text is built up and the range of shared meanings is expanded, it becomes unnecessary for every component of meaning to be explicitly mentioned again and again. For once things start to become obvious, they can either be left for the reader or listener to guess, or they can be hinted at by short words which substitute for the precise expression. This avoidance of needless repetition is common enough in written texts, but it is even more obvious in conversation, where there is constant interaction between the speakers.

There are two closely related devices to consider here: **ellipsis**, where something is left out altogether, and **substitution**, where something is replaced by a substitute. These devices are like reference in their effect — they form links between two parts of a text — but they operate in a different way. Reference establishes a meaning relationship directly, whereas ellipsis and substitution do so indirectly by assuming the completion of particular grammatical structures.

Ellipsis and substitution are both very common in classroom interaction between teacher and students. Here is an example of ellipsis:

> TEACHER: What do they use their tongues for?
> CHILD: Smelling.

The child answers with one word. Everything else the child might have said (e.g. *They use their tongues for* . . .) has already been said in the teacher's question and so the child can take it for granted. The question hinges on the *what* and that is what the child responds to. This type of answer is very common in many situations, not only in classroom interaction. Some teachers try to insist on children giving 'full sentence answers' but questions of this type do not need them.

Ellipsis can also occur within one speaker's text, as this extract from a radio report demonstrates:

> Peace talks were set to resume today if the truce held. It didn't and they haven't.

The full second sentence would have been: *It didn't hold and they haven't resumed today.* But what's left out can easily be recovered from the previous sentence, even though it's in a different form there. A more extensive ellipsis occurs in the sound track of the film *Breakfast at Tiffany's*:

> I've never had champagne before breakfast before. With breakfast, often. But never before before.

Ellipsis on a small scale is so common in written texts that it's seldom noticed. In the next example only the word *read* is omitted (twice):

> people who read because they choose to, not because they have to

However, in writing as in speech, ellipsis can also be used more noticeably for rhetorical effect. In the following example it sharpens the impact of the final sentence:

> His negotiations can be remarkably specific. When he agreed to appear in a night club in Parramatta, his contract specified that if his heavily pregnant wife was about to give birth, he would pull out. She was and he did.

We'll turn now to an example of substitution:

> CHILD: I liked the big snake.
> TEACHER: The big one.
> CHILD: Yes.

Here the teacher repeats the noun group from the child's statement, but it is not a word-for-word repetition: *one* is substituted for the head noun of the group to avoid unnecessary repetition. (*One* is the word most commonly substituted for the head noun.) The child's further response is an example of ellipsis; *yes* represents the whole clause *I liked the big snake*.

The next example is taken from a conversation between two girls about eleven years old. It includes examples of both substitution and ellipsis, as well as one example of reference:

A: I couldn't imagine being a teacher.

B: No. I could imagine being a dancing teacher.

(No ellipsis or substitution, but a further qualification.)

A: I could, 'cause I'm going to be one.

(Ellipsis of imagine being a dancing teacher. *Substitution of* one *for* a dancing teacher.)

B: So am I.

(Substitution of so *for* going to be one, *with additional meaning of 'and also'. Note that* one *is a substitution itself; note too the inverted word order following* so *as theme.)*

A: Either that or a secretary.

(Ellipsis of I'm going to be. *Reference to* a dancing teacher *via* that.)

We can illustrate both reference and substitution by amending this well-known tongue twister:

Peter Piper picked a peck of pickled pepper.
If Peter Piper picked a peck of pickled pepper,
Where's the peck of pickled pepper Peter Piper picked?

Some modification can save the tongue several twists:

Peter Piper picked a peck of pickled pepper.
If he did so,
Where is it?

While we would have to admit that this second version completely misses the point, it does not lose its essential meaning. The first line is all New information. In lines 2 and 3 the Given information is taken care of by the reference pronouns *he* and *it* and by the substitution *did so*.

Lexical cohesion

The sense of cohesion in a text can also be established by the lexical items — that is, by the words in the text and the semantic relationships amongst them. These relationships, together with those marked by the grammatical devices of reference, allow groups of words in a text to be seen as forming **chains** by which most of the sentences are linked. The main types of relationship are set out overleaf.

Repetition   Some words may simply be repeated several times to refer to the same thing or things at different points in the text.

Synonymy   Two different words with the same meaning are referred to as *synonyms*. It is sometimes said that no two words can have exactly the same meaning and so there are no true synonyms. However, many pairs of words are so close in meaning that they are effectively synonyms, even if they are not interchangeable in every context. Furthermore, in any particular text, it may be obvious that two synonyms refer to the same thing.

Antonymy   Words that are opposite in meaning are referred to as *antonyms*. There are several kinds of antonymy, though they can all operate as cohesive devices. Gradable antonymy, where the two terms are relative, applies to pairs like *old* and *new*, or *large* and *small* (a small elephant is not a small animal, even though an elephant is an animal). Non-gradable antonymy applies to opposed pairs like *dead* or *alive*, and *male* or *female*, where there are no shades of difference in between — at least not in the everyday sense of the terms. Very similar is the relationship of converse pairs like *husband* and *wife*, or *buy* and *sell*, where the one depends on the existence of the other.

Hyponymy   This is the relationship of members of a class to the whole class. So *elephant, tiger, leopard* and *deer* are hyponyms of the term *animal*. Hyponymy is a relationship of inclusion and depends on how things are classified.

Meronymy   This is the part-whole relationship. To continue with the animal examples, *trunk, leg, tail* and *ear* are all meronyms of *elephant*. Meronymy is a relationship of composition and depends on what things are made up of.

Collocation   There are words which typically occur in the same context and which can therefore be regarded as being related to each other — for example, *cook . . . stove . . . oven . . . bake*. This relationship is sometimes referred to as *collocation* (a term also used to refer to standard pairings like *fish and chips* which we discussed in Chapter 7). However, collocation is not itself a precise relationship, though it may include more precise relationships like those described above.

Most of these relationships are to be found in the text which follows.

TEXT 12.1 EXTRACT FROM A MAGAZINE ARTICLE ON CRIME RATES

Crime rates also vary within countries and between different parts of the same society. The Northern Territory has by far the highest murder rate in Australia. The risk of death by homicide is much higher for unskilled workers than it is for professionals, and homicide is many times more common among Aborigines than other groups of Australians.

Violent crime needs also to be viewed in the context of other causes of death and injury. For every homicide in Australia there are about three deaths from accidental falls, six suicides, nine road fatalities and about 60 deaths related to smoking.

Trends in non-fatal violent crime have to be interpreted cautiously. Technological developments have improved crime records, and because of shifting social attitudes — often reflected in legislative changes — it is now generally considered that many more crimes involving sexual assault and domestic violence are reported today than were reported a decade or two ago. So the trend in these crime rates may exaggerate the degree to which there has been a true increase in violent crime. How much of the recent rise in violent crimes (other than murder) is real, and how much a statistical artefact, we simply do not know.

In this text lexical cohesion is established partly by the series of noun groups. They are shown in the diagram below with some important connections drawn in.

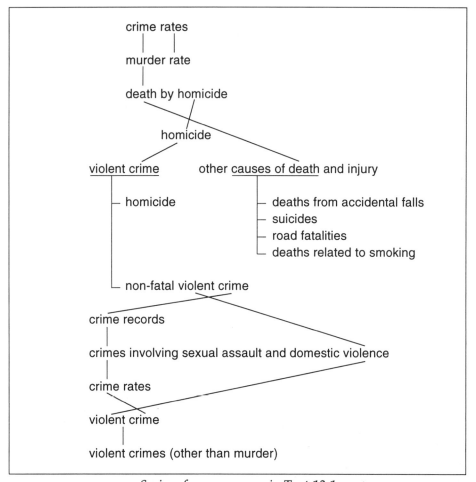

Series of noun groups in Text 12.1

In this series we can identity a 'crime' chain involving many repetitions of the word *crime* itself and other words which are hyponyms of *crime* — namely, *homicide* and *murder*. The noun group *death by homicide* introduces a related chain with repetitions of the word *death*, a synonym *fatalities* and a hyponym *suicide*.

In the noun groups in which the word *crime* occurs, we find it sometimes as the head noun of the group:

> violent crime
>
> non-fatal violent crime
>
> crimes involving sexual assault and domestic violence
>
> violent crimes (other than murder)

In other groups, *crime* (or its hyponym *murder*) is a classifier:

> crime rates
>
> murder rate
>
> crime records

This allows another chain, based on *rates*, to be linked with the 'crime' chain, a link which is established from the first theme in the text. This 'rates' chain also involves words like *trends* and *statistical* (and more peripherally *risk*, *reported* and *interpreted*).

There are also some minor chains. For example, in the first paragraph we have *countries*, with *Australia* as a hyponym and with *the Northern Territory* as a meronym of *Australia*. The word *countries* is also, taken in a slightly different sense, a synonym of *society*. In this sense it is related to two meronymic pairs in the same paragraph: *unskilled workers/professionals* and *Aborigines/other groups of Australians*. All these chains of lexical items with specifiable relationships help to establish cohesion within the text.

Conjunction

Another major device for holding text together is **conjunction**. We have already discussed some aspects of this — the way clauses are held together within the one sentence — in dealing with complex messages in Chapter 9. But conjunction also operates across sentence boundaries, showing how pairs of sentences or a whole series of sentences are related together. Conjunction is thus one of the ways in which the structure of the whole text is built up.

The term *conjunction* refers to a relationship: that is, to some kind of connection between elements within a text, either within the one sentence or amongst a group of sentences. It also refers to the class of words, word groups and phrases which can be used signal those connections and make them explicit. Sometimes, of course, they are left implicit (i.e. no word or phrase is used to signal the relationship).

There are several different kinds of conjunctive relationship. The four main ones can be summed up in these words: *and*, *then*, *so*, *but*. They are briefly explained below, with further examples of conjunctions, especially those commonly used to link larger elements in the text.

Additive *(and)* The additive relationship, which essentially joins elements together, is likely to occur in any text. Typical conjunctions include:

> and, and also
>
> furthermore, in addition, besides
>
> or, or else
>
> nor, and . . . not

Temporal *(then)* In narratives and other texts organised in a time sequence, temporal conjunctions are often used to make the time relationships explicit. Examples include:

> then, after that, subsequently   first of all
>
> just then, at the same time   next, secondly
>
> previously, before that   finally, in conclusion
>
> soon, (an hour) later
>
> meanwhile

Some of these conjunctions, especially those in the right-hand column, can also be used to mark sequences within a text (e.g. a sequence of arguments).

Causal *(so)* Texts involving explanations, arguments, discussions and so on often include causal relationships. They are typically marked by conjunctions such as:

> so, then, hence, therefore, for
>
> consequently, accordingly, because of this
>
> for this reason, as a result
>
> with this in mind

Adversative *(but)* Ideas are sometimes presented as contrasting or opposed to one another. Conjunctions which commonly mark this include:

> but, yet, though
>
> however, on the other hand
>
> nevertheless, none the less, despite this

These four are the main relationships, but there are a few others, including:

Continuatives These allow the speaker or writer to signal that he or she is pressing on with the text. They are particularly appropriate in spoken English — especially in conversation, where it is often necessary to signal that you intend to continue speaking. Common examples are:

now   of course   well   anyway   surely   after all

Intonation   This device can also be used to establish relationships between sentences, but only in spoken texts of course.

The following text, an official letter, includes examples of some of these types of conjunction:

Dear Contributor,

The State Government has legislated for the introduction of a Health Insurance Levy to provide for free ambulance service to people contributing to a basic hospital fund. Following a challenge to this legislation by the Commonwealth Government, the Australian High Court has now determined that the legislation is valid. Consequently, the ambulance levy will be effective from 1 February 1983 and will replace the Ambulance Contribution Scheme.

As a result payments to the Ambulance Contribution Scheme will no longer be necessary. Benefits will now be available through contributions to basic hospital insurance with a registered health fund.

As your current ambulance contribution is financial beyond 1 February 1983, a refund of the unavailable period is due to you and accordingly your cheque is enclosed herewith.

In this letter we have examples of marked relationships both within sentences and between sentences. In the first of the following two sentences we see a temporal relationship illustrated, and in the second two causal relationships :

Following a challenge to this legislation . . . , the Australian High Court has now determined . . .

As your current ambulance contribution is financial . . . , a refund of the unavailable period is due to you and accordingly your cheque . . .

But the focus of this chapter is cohesion in the larger text, and in this text we have two examples of cohesion established by conjunction. They are both specifically concerned with consequence:

Consequently, the ambulance levy will be effective from 1 February 1983 and will replace . . .

As a result payments to the Ambulance Contribution Scheme will no longer be necessary.

The word *consequently* and the phrase *as a result* each show how their sentences are related to what has gone before.

The whole text

The cohesive devices we have surveyed in this chapter play an important part in establishing a text as an interconnected whole. For, as we have remarked earlier, the grammatical devices by which sentences are linked together help to show that they do form a text. Of course it is also possible to consider the structure of the text as a whole, but this would take us beyond the scope of grammar.

However, we can remark here that there are many different purposes for texts which entail different genres, and that these differences are evident in the grammatical structures used in the texts. So a text like a recount or a narrative, where events are related in a time sequence, will be likely to have a certain range of grammatical structures. Whereas a text in another genre — say a set of instructions or a political argument — will typically have different grammatical structures. The same goes for spoken texts — a conversation amongst several people making arrangements for something they are going to do will have a different grammar from an academic lecture. The kind of grammar relates directly to the purpose and helps to make clear what the purpose is.

Grammar is an integral part of language and the study of grammar should be closely related to other aspects of language study and to the uses of language in the life of the wider community.

Grammar in the Classroom

It is not the intention of this book to tell you in detail what to do about grammar in the classroom. That would require another book — at least. However, this Postscript will explore some of the ways in which the grammar we've surveyed is relevant to teachers and their students as they go about learning to use English effectively.

Why should grammar be taught?

In the teaching of English in recent times, the prevailing assumption has been that it is much more important for students to be able to use their language effectively than for them to know much about the language and its grammatical structures. The all-important aim has been competence in language use. We have also emphasised the wholeness of language and resisted breaking it down into parts for study and analysis. This has been associated with a quite proper recognition of the close relationships amongst all the modes of language (speaking, listening, etc.) and their integration with all the other activities of the curriculum.

However, one of the assumptions lying behind this book is that it is possible for students not only to develop their competence in using language, but also to gain some understanding of what language is like and how it works. Moreover, it is possible to pay attention to details of grammatical structure without losing sight of the overall purpose and structure of the texts under consideration. Since the functional approach is based on the functions and meanings involved, it allows us to make direct connections between the local details of language and the whole text and its context. Coming to an understanding of how language works in this way is likely to increase our students' competence in using it.

Even without explicit teaching, children do learn some things about language as they continue to use it. Early on they notice features of language, such as particular words, different accents and so on — and from time to time they comment on these things. Once they begin to develop their literacy, they learn about language in more specific ways. The processes of learning to read and write are inevitably processes of learning about language. Learning to handle a writing system like our alphabet involves some analysis of the spoken language that the learners are already familiar with. And as children learn to read — no matter how this occurs — they not only learn about speech sounds and their relationship to letters, but they also learn to recognise words for what they are and begin to learn about sentences.

Where children have the opportunity to learn another language (whether they are learning English as a second language, or learning a language in addition to English), they are learning all sorts of things about their first language through the comparisons that must inevitably be made. Moreover, this kind of learning is much more focused on the lexico-grammatical organisation of language than is initial literacy learning. So, as children encounter and explore the systems of a new language, they also learn something about the equivalent systems of their first language.

Undoubtedly some aspects of the grammatical system of a new language do need to be taught, and for this reason we should be aware of the special needs of ESL learners. There are several aspects of English which native speakers might deal with more or less automatically (once they have reached the level of competence gained in early childhood), but which might not be so easy for people from a different language background. In other words, some ESL learners may have to learn explicitly how to do things that native speakers appear to pick up simply through having more extensive experience — things such as how questions are formed and other structures where word order is crucial for the meaning, which are discussed in Chapter 3. However, this does not mean that teachers should provide full-on grammar lessons for ESL students. What it does mean is that they should have a good understanding of the grammatical features of English which their students are coming to grips with.

Yet even native speakers need to be aware of some aspects of the grammar of their language. One may ask, 'How conscious are we of the grammar when we are using the language?' In answering this question, we can draw a contrast between two extremes. On the one hand, there are areas like the grammar of everyday conversation: for example, forming negatives or tag questions. This area is highly rule-governed and native speakers all learn the established patterns in early childhood. However, most people don't know about it except in the most general terms (e.g. question, statement, negative, etc.). And for ordinary purposes they don't need to know about it. On the other hand — at the other extreme — there are some areas of grammar where to be conscious of it can help us to control it. This applies especially to some aspects of writing, which for the most part is not learnt in early childhood but in the more formal learning contexts of school. Such features as how we relate clauses together, or how items are referred to in successive parts of a written text, or features relating to the overall organisation and cohesion of written texts in particular genres, need to be taught explicitly even to most native speakers. These are often areas where the writer has some choice, and they are not matters about which anyone can give a simple ruling — right or wrong. They are matters of judgement. This is where it is important for children to learn about the grammar.

If students understand something of the detailed texture and local requirements at various points of a text, they will be able to marshal the resources of their language more effectively. They will also have the terms to enable them to discuss their language use amongst themselves and with their teachers. The main point is that if students have some understanding how their language works, they will be able to speak and write with more control and confidence for all the various purposes for which they need to use language.

How should grammar be taught?

We should begin by asking how people learn their first language. As children grow through the pre-school and early school years, how do they learn to use the grammatical structures and conventions and how do they learn the vocabulary? For the most part, they do not develop their command of grammar by learning rules or their vocabulary from words presented to them in lists. These things develop essentially through experience — through all of the children's experiences of language, both spoken and written, in every area of life. However, if children are getting the kind of experience which nourishes their language development, then it is useful for teachers to draw attention to specific features of the language, especially where they can be related to the broader contexts of meaning which the children are engaged with. Children are more likely to gain control of sentence structure and other grammatical features (and the associated punctuation) when they learn about them in the context of texts they are writing, rather than through exercises dealing with isolated items.

In the days when grammar was taught in schools on a regular and systematic basis, teaching about language was usually rather detached from students' uses of language in activities like written expression or oral English lessons. This detachment from meaningful contexts and uses applied even to those prescriptive aspects of grammar teaching which were intended to influence students' usage, such as exercises where they had to correct sentences. However, in a functional approach to language, it is essential for learning about language to be integrated with the students' own uses of language and related to texts which can be seen in a larger context. This means that much of the grammar will be introduced in lessons where the main focus will be on other things — often on some aspect of the students' writing. The emphasis may still be on the students' learning to use their language, but within that context they can also be learning something about the language involved. This learning can begin in a modest way at the kindergarten level, where some obvious patterns of words and sounds (e.g. rhyming) can be noted. Then, as the students continue to develop their writing and other modes as they move through the grades, they can go further in learning about the systems of their language.

All this may suggest that any explicit discussion of grammatical points should be based on written language, and especially on the students' own writing. Admittedly written text does have an advantage: it is there on the page and you can focus on it without losing it. But if students are used to taking account of grammatical structures and if the development of their oral language is not just left to chance, it too will provide opportunities for some focus on the language involved — perhaps captured on a tape recorder. The most important point here is for students to get used to changing their focus. At times the focus will be on using language (reading, writing, speaking, listening) in order to achieve whatever goals are relevant at that moment. At other times, within this general approach, there can be a focus on some specific aspect of language, such as a grammatical structure that's being used. The change of focus can be compared with zooming in on a visual image and then out again. Once the capacity to shift focus is established, there is scope for some more systematic teaching about language, partly to consolidate understanding of technical terms, such as *clause* or *verb group*, and partly to develop a framework of understanding, so that students see the grammar as part of an interrelated system.

There is always a temptation with grammar to give all the attention to the system itself — the forms and structures and how they are related to each other — and to forget about why these forms exist or how they function in real uses of language. This was one problem with the traditional practice of teaching grammar via exercises unrelated to — and sometimes in conflict with — actual uses of language. On the other hand, if the grammar is firmly anchored in the texts the students are using and producing and related to the wider context, it is more likely that they will be able to see how it works and why they are considering it.

But even when the texts under consideration are clearly related to their context and purpose, there is a risk that the grammar can become detached from the reality. For example, if we are talking with students about the features of the recount genre, we may mention that it typically uses the past tense. But why is that significant? It is much more likely to be seen as significant if we are comparing it with another genre like report, which typically uses the simple non-past (present) tense. For the tense difference is associated with other differences in meaning. Recounts commonly deal with specific events which can be located in time, namely in the past. Reports typically deal with generalisations where time is not relevant, and for them we use the 'timeless present'. This particular choice is most evident in material processes in those parts of the report where actions or typical behaviour are being presented (relational processes typically have the simple form present anyway).

Another genre where types of process may vary is narrative. In a story that focuses mainly on external actions, material processes will predominate, while if the thoughts and feelings of the characters are important, there will be many mental and verbal processes. Thus the grammar can be associated with more general features, such as how the story is being presented. Student writers can discuss these possibilities and explore them in their own reading and writing; in any case the grammar should be linked to the broader meaning.

Once a climate has been generated in the classroom where such features of language are matters of general discussion, it's possible to focus more attention on the language system itself and begin to build up a framework of grammatical understandings, which can be developed as students move through the various stages of learning in primary school and on into the secondary school. Sometimes of course the focus can be shifted back onto details of the grammar itself, and some points may be dealt with in brief mini-lessons.

Why functional grammar?

What is different about the functional approach? Are we 'going back' to grammar or taking on something new? The most important characteristic of functional grammar is that it is closely related to the meanings being expressed through language. Thus its concern is not just with different kinds of words and structures, but with features of the language that reflect and gain their meanings from the purpose and overall meaning of the text. These connections with context and purpose mean that there are criteria available for evaluating language realistically.

By contrast, in the traditional teaching of grammar, there was a pre-occupation with what was correct and with establishing in all students' usage a particular kind of English — often conceived in terms of relatively trivial details like the pseudo-problem of the 'split infinitive'. Teachers concentrated on detail and gave little or no attention to the overall shape of texts, or whether they achieved their purposes or not. As a result some aspects of traditional grammar teaching were very prescriptive (even though it was also partly descriptive), and students were given the idea that one kind of English was correct, while any deviation from that was wrong. Moreover, because of the focus on fine details, many students did not gain any grasp of the overall organisation of texts or how they could be organised for particular purposes. And many, particularly those who did not use standard forms of English, were inclined to have a low regard for their own use of English; they were so afraid of making a mistake that they were unable to use it with confidence to achieve their own purposes. Discouraged from speaking and writing, they had little opportunity to practise.

The functional approach to language recognises that English is richly varied and that most people have some contact with several varieties of English. Moreover, the variations are themselves functional, so that on some occasions it will be appropriate to use one rather than another. There are also significant functional differences between written and spoken language which students must come to terms with if they are to learn to write effectively. Such differences include the issue of nominalisation, discussed at the end of Chapter 7. In certain kinds of written English there are advantages in nominalisation. Yet there are dangers as well; if writing departs too far from speech, it runs the risk of being inaccessible to all but the most experienced readers.

Another legacy of traditional grammar is the folklore that has developed about how to improve the quality of a piece of writing. One element of this is the 'chuck in a few adjectives' solution. Some teachers regularly advise students to 'use lots of adjectives' as a recipe for making writing more interesting. (In some classrooms and some textbooks in the past, there were even exercises in which students had to take a sentence and 'make it more interesting' by adding a phrase or two, an adverb and of course lots of adjectives.) There is an assumption here that adjectives are the key to good writing. There may also be a hidden assumption that adjectives are optional extras, mere decoration and not essential to the message. A more functional position is to recognise that adjectives are often necessary, that they have several useful roles (e.g. as epithets and classifiers) and that they can be overdone; prose 'overgrown with adjectives and adverbs' is unlikely to be an improvement. Much the same can be said of 'good sentence openings'. As mentioned in Chapter 11, these often involve marked themes, which can play a very important role in a text. Yet they too can be overdone — in fact they can change the whole emphasis of the text — and it is better to get students to examine the thematic development of their texts as a whole.

What about the technical terms?

What we need, essentially, is a set of terms which provides us with a 'language for talking about language', at one level for talking with colleagues and at another level for talking with our students. But does a functional model of language mean that we should no longer use terms such as *noun*, *verb* and *adjective*? The short answer is no, because much of traditional grammar is included in functional grammar. Although there are significant differences, there is no great gulf between them. So, while the functional model brings with it a number of new terms, many of the traditional terms are used as well. The new ones are introduced especially for concepts not recognised in traditional grammar: for example, the functional components of the clause — processes, participants and circumstances. We have seen that the structure which represents the process is the verb group, and yet in many clauses the verb group consists simply of a single verb. So for simplicity's sake we may refer to the process as 'the verb'. But we must remember that the term *verb* really refers to a class of words, whereas process refers to a kind of meaning; it is a functional component in the clause based on the role that part of the clause is fulfilling.

In traditional grammar there is a tendency to concentrate on identifying and classifying the formal elements of a language; a functional grammar is more concerned with how the language works to achieve various purposes. Traditional grammar often begins with words and other small elements of the language and works up to the larger structures, whereas a functional grammar focuses first on the larger grammatical components and their functions within texts. The traditional 'parts of speech' (or a similar classification of words) have a place in a functional approach, but they must be seen in relation to larger functional components which can be directly related to the meanings being expressed. It is still appropriate to talk about nouns, verbs and other kinds of words (and to use those traditional terms), but they are not the most crucial units. More important are units at the level of clause and sentence and how they are deployed in a text. It is at this level that meanings and their wording are more consciously considered and where decisions about wording and punctuation are made.

*   *   *   *   *

Language is best learnt in the context of actual language use. When it comes to grammar, the most important point is to maintain the links between learning to use the language and learning about the language, so that we are not trying to achieve one without the other. This can be managed by locating any early attention to grammar in contexts where the students are using their language with interest and engagement. Then there can be a shift of focus — zooming in and out again — so that the language features are noted without losing sight of the overall context and purpose. Once the students get used to this practice, the teacher can go further, dealing with the grammar more systematically so as to develop a broad framework of understanding. Many good teachers are already doing a great deal of this and so, rather than having to make a radical change, you may simply need to enhance your existing practice. The main thing is to equip all your students with both the competence and the understanding to achieve everything they need to use language for.

Bibliography

Major sources

Halliday, M. A. K. 1985, *An Introduction to Functional Grammar*, Edward Arnold, London (revised edition in press).

Halliday, M. A. K. and Hasan, R. 1976, *Cohesion in English*, Longman, London.

Quirk, R., Greenbaum, S., Leech, G. and Svartvik, J. 1985, *A Comprehensive Grammar of the English Language*, Longman, London (a massive reference book, but Chapter 2 is a 60-page survey of modern English grammar).

Further reading

References marked with an asterisk are suggested starting points for teachers.

*Christie, F. et al. 1990–92, *Language: A Resource for Meaning*: Teacher's Books for *Exploring Procedures*, *Exploring Reports* and *Exploring Explanations*, Harcourt Brace Jovanovich, Sydney.

*Collerson, J. 1990, *Grammar*, Parts 1 & 2, PENs 77 & 78, PETA, Sydney.

*Cusworth, R. 1994, *What Is a Functional Model of Language?*, PEN 95, PETA, Sydney.

*Derewianka, B. 1990, *Exploring How Texts Work*, PETA, Sydney.

Eggins, S. 1994, *An Introduction to Systemic Functional Linguistics*, Pinter, London.

Garner, M. 1983, *Grammar: Warts and All*, River Seine, Melbourne (mainly traditional).

Gerot, L. and Wignell, P. (in press), *Making Sense of Functional Grammar*, AEE, Sydney.

Greenbaum, S. 1991, *An Introduction to English Grammar*, Longman, London (an outline of modern grammar with sections on punctuation, usage and spelling).

*Halliday, M. A. K. 1985, *Spoken and Written Language*, Deakin University Press, Geelong (an accessible work based on a functional approach).

Huddleston, R. 1988, *English Grammar: An Outline*, Cambridge University Press, Cambridge (a modern grammar).

*Knapp, P. and Watkins, M. 1994, *Context – Text – Grammar: Teaching the Genres and Grammar of School Writing in Infants and Primary Classrooms*, Text Productions, Sydney.

Leech, G. and Svartvik, J. 1975, *A Communicative Grammar of English*, Longman, London (incorporates some functional notions; revised edition in press).

Martin, J. R. 1992, *English Text: System and Structure*, John Benjamins, Philadelphia & Amsterdam (an advanced and detailed treatment in the functional tradition).

Swan, M. 1980, *Practical English Usage*, Oxford University Press, Oxford (a reference book on modern English grammar and usage).

*Williams, G. 1993, 'Using systemic grammar in teaching young learners: an introduction', in L. Unsworth (ed.), *Literacy Learning and Teaching: Language as Social Practice in the Primary School*, Macmillan, Melbourne.

Index